Praise for *You're Addicted to You*

"Through examples that will have you nodding your head as you recognize yourself, *You're Addicted to You* shines a light on common self-addictions and helps you identify your own. Blumenthal's realistic, systems approach for tackling personal and professional change can help you get started on a new quest or sustain changes already underway."

> —Tammy J. Winnie, Director,
> Global Organization Effectiveness, Kellogg Company

"My life's work has been helping people overcome self-reinforcing and self-defeating behaviors. Noah Blumenthal understands how to do this and after reading this book you will too."

> —James O. Prochaska, PhD, author of *Changing for Good*

"In this engaging and informed guide to enhancing self-awareness and personal growth, Noah Blumenthal helps us to find effective pathways to change. You will recognize many people in his examples, most importantly, yourself. And you'll start to apply what you learn before day's end. Blumenthal will get you going. Beyond that, as he makes clear, anything is possible . . . it's up to you."

> — Joseph G. Cunningham, PhD,
> Professor of Psychology, Brandeis University

"With all the attention our culture invests in advice for every kind of personal change—from weight loss to leadership style—it's striking how little genuine wisdom we have for how to change once we've identified what to change. In *You're Addicted to You*, Noah Blumenthal offers concrete, effective strategies for finding traction to change where change has eluded you before."

> — Keith Allred, Faculty Member, Kennedy School of
> Government, Harvard University
> Founder, TheCommonInterest.o

"Noah Blumenthal has created a simple, yet powerful means for effecting personal change. In an era where everything is supposed to be quicker and more automated, it is refreshing to find an approach that both honors the struggle we all face and acknowledges the time needed to make real, lasting changes to our behavior."

— Ethan Schutz, President, Business Consultants Network

"Noah Blumenthal has crafted a book for self-improvement that seems to have been personally written for each of its readers. It is an excellent guide toward the achievement of a happy life and the rediscovery of the divinity that resides in all of us. I am excited for the life-affirming opportunities that this approach can bring to my work and to my home."

— Rabbi Mark Covitz, Congregation Beth Yam,
Hilton Head Island, South Carolina

"Anyone who has tried to change knows how difficult it can be. Noah Blumenthal provides not only a voice of encouragement and optimism, but provides concrete tools we can use immediately to transform the lead of present circumstances into future gold."

— Karlin Sloan, CEO, Karlin Sloan & Company

"*You're Addicted to You* addresses a problem familiar to the diverse worlds of health psychology, organizational change, and individual counseling: how does one facilitate real behavior change, change which endures for more than a very brief time? Noah presents the possibility of change using straightforward language, helpful examples, assessment tools, and homework."

— Kathleen M. Schiaffino, PhD,
Associate Professor of Psychology, Fordham University

You're Addicted to YOU

You're Addicted to YOU

Why It's So
Hard to Change—and
**What You Can
Do About It**

Noah Blumenthal

BK

BERRETT-KOEHLER PUBLISHERS, INC.
San Francisco
a BK Life book

Berrett-Koehler Publishers, Inc.
235 Montgomery Street, Suite 650
San Francisco, CA 94104-2916
Tel: (415) 288-0260 Fax: (415) 362-2512 www.bkconnection.com

Ordering Information

Quantity sales. Special discounts are available on quantity purchases by corporations,
associations, and others. For details, contact the "Special Sales Department" at the Berrett-
Koehler address above.
Individual sales. Berrett-Koehler publications are available through most bookstores. They
can also be ordered directly from Berrett-Koehler. Tel: (800) 929-2929; Fax: (802) 864-7626;
www.bkconnection.com
Orders for college textbook/course adoption use. Please contact Berrett-Koehler.
Tel: (800) 929-2929; Fax: (802) 864-7626.
Orders by U.S. trade bookstores and wholesalers. Please contact Publishers Group West,
1700 Fourth Street, Berkeley, CA 94710. Tel: (510) 528-1444; Fax (510) 528-3444.

Berrett-Koehler and the BK logo are registered trademarks of Berrett-Koehler Publishers, Inc.

Printed in the United States of America

Berrett-Koehler books are printed on long-lasting acid-free paper. When it is available,
we choose paper that has been manufactured by environmentally responsible processes.
These may include using trees grown in sustainable forests, incorporating recycled paper,
minimizing chlorine in bleaching, or recycling the energy produced at the paper mill.

Library of Congress Cataloging-in-Publication Data
Blumenthal, Noah, 1972–
    You're addicted to you : why it's so hard to change and what you can do about it / Noah
Blumenthal.
        p.   cm.
    ISBN: 978-1-57675-427-6 (pbk.)
1. Change (Psychology) 2. Change (Psychology)--Problems, exercises, etc. I. Title. II. Title:
You are addicted to you.
    BF637.C4B56 2007
    158.1—dc22   2006100740

First Edition

12 11 10 09 08 07   10 9 8 7 6 5 4 3 2 1

Text design by Detta Penna

To my wife Beatrice,
who has supported me
and believed in me
and helped me find my laughter.

Contents

Preface

I wrote this book because too many people believe that change is a matter of willpower. They believe that if people want to make significant changes in their lives, those with greater willpower will be successful. Those who fail to change do so because they lack something internally. They just don't have the drive or conviction to see their efforts through.

The truth is we are all capable of changing ourselves. The problem is we are constantly bombarded with recommendations on *what* to change, but never really taught *how* to make difficult changes. We are told what we should change by friends and family, bosses and coworkers, magazines and TV shows, but then we are left without guidance. Once we know what results we want, how do we go about ridding ourselves of the bad habits we have accumulated over the course of our lives, and how do we replace those old behaviors with the new, superior ones? This book will help you identify what change or changes you want to make in yourself, and then it will answer the question of "how?"

Early in my career I watched one of my employers send hundreds of managers off to leadership training. The participants raved that it was, " a life-changing experience," and spoke of the program in reverent tones. However, in the weeks and months following their return from the program, it was pretty clear that little or no change had taken place. They treated their staff the same way they did prior to the training. The same went for how they managed their work, talked about the business, responded to crises, and "led" their organization.

The company must have spent millions of dollars on this training effort and the participants claimed that it was worth every penny. Unfortunately, no one changed. I saw the same thing happen in my personal world. Friends wanted to change their work habits, how they ate or exercised, or how they communicated with their spouses.

They had the best intentions and strong motivation, but they almost always failed to make good on their plans.

I don't think these people lacked willpower or desire. I truly believe they all wanted to change and that they even knew what they wanted that change to be. They wanted to be thinner, healthier, more considerate of others, more diligent, or better leaders. They just didn't have a process to guide them through their change. The only advice they received was, "try harder."

This book gives you a concrete process with nine clear steps to help you make your change. It is born out of both my professional and educational experiences. As an executive coach, I have helped hundreds of corporate clients, business owners, salespeople, and various individuals make difficult changes. I've helped them make changes to their leadership style, the effectiveness of their communication and relationships, the control they have over their emotions, and many other areas. As an undergraduate student in psychology and then as a graduate student in organizational psychology, I studied personal change and resistance and learned how a clear and effective process can greatly improve an individual's ability to change.

I have watched real people succeed and fail at change and I have studied the topic at length. The conclusion I have drawn is that people need a new model for understanding how to change themselves. I use the concept of self-addiction—that people are addicted to their own behaviors. Being addicted to your behaviors doesn't make you a bad person. You may be an exceptional parent, spouse, manager, and/or leader, but even the best will sometimes struggle with change and improvement. We all have something we could change to make ourselves happier, more effective, and more fulfilled in life and in work.

Using the concept of addiction is not meant to equate the behavioral challenges I will discuss in this book with the hereditary, biological, and chemical challenges of drug or alcohol addictions. This book is not meant as a treatment for, nor in any way to make light of, those diseases. However, the concept of addiction is important because it puts personal change into a new context. This book honestly states how difficult change is and gives you a real path to create that change.

How should you use this book?

If you have read this far, then you probably want to either change something in your life or help someone else in their change. You may have a specific change in mind, or perhaps you know that you wish to improve yourself in some way but haven't yet figured out exactly what that improvement is. In either case, this book can help you make any change you want to make. You can use it on its own or to help you implement something you learned in another book. If you don't already know what you want to change, it will help you identify that. Then it will give you the key to answering the question of **how** to make that change.

This is not a traditional book that is meant to be read cover to cover in a couple of days. There are exercises throughout this book that ask you to stop, think, and take concrete action. I recommend that you complete these activities as you go. Sometimes you may feel the need to redo prior exercises and/or reread prior chapters. Change does not follow a single path, nor does it follow a consistent timeline. You may complete this book and reach the final stages of maintaining your change within a couple of weeks. Alternatively, you could spend months actively working on one change; it all depends on the strength of your self-addiction and the effort—the commitment and energy—you put into the change.

As you complete the exercises in this book, you will be asked to record various thoughts, commitments, actions, and observations. I recommend you record all these items in one location so that you can easily review them on a regular basis. You can purchase a notebook specifically for this purpose.

What will you find in this book?

In the following pages you will find answers to three main questions:

1. What is a self-addiction?
2. What are some of your self-addictions?
3. How do you conquer these behaviors?

The strategies that are proposed in this book for how to conquer these behaviors are broken down into three parts: Raising Awareness, Building Support, and Taking Action.

Raising Awareness

This section is the foundation for your change. It begins with understanding your current behaviors and identifying your self-addictions. It then guides you through realizing the impact of your behavior on you and those around you, which leads you to the critical step of making a powerful commitment that will drive the behaviors to make you successful in your change.

Building Support

This section helps you identify and draw strength from a network of people who will support you in your change efforts. The value comes not just from surrounding yourself with people who will support you, but in clearly defining how each of those people can support your change. Bringing others in and engaging them to help you will make your change efforts far more effective. The Building Support section provides you with strategies that will help you find, develop, and maintain effective support relationships.

Taking Action

This section presents three types of actions that you can use to make your change: one for practicing new behaviors, one for reminding yourself to avoid engaging in old behaviors, and one for reviewing your progress. The routines you create will provide a consistency of action that will help you conquer your self-addiction.

To better understand these processes, you are introduced to *The Talker, The Pushover, The Worker,* and *The Critic.* Each of these individuals has gone through his or her own change process to overcome self-addiction. These characters are composites of many people I have known as clients, colleagues, friends, and family. Of course, I'd be lying if I said that the characters didn't also have a little of me in them. However, they are not intended to depict anyone specifically; rather, they are intended to give you a glimpse into some of the experiences people can have as they work to change themselves. I hope you find them illustrative, encouraging, and even motivational. Most of all, I hope they help you develop the confidence, strength, and know-how to make your change.

Finally, you are introduced to a gentleman I met when he became my client. I have since come to consider him a friend. He is a recovering alcoholic and a strong proponent of Alcoholics Anonymous (AA). I share bits of his story, not to equate alcoholism with self-addiction, but because we can learn valuable lessons from the success that AA has had over the years.

I wrote this book to provide a process to help people change. Just think what you could do with a system that guides you to identify valuable changes you need to make in your life, make those changes effectively, and then sustain them over time. I truly believe that anyone can change, and I wish you luck in making your change journey exciting, rewarding, fun and, most of all, successful.

Noah Blumenthal
December 2006

P. S. As you read this book, you can also join the change community online. Share your success stories, challenges, tips, and lessons you've learned in the Virtual Partners Forum at www.YoureAddictedToYou.com.

Acknowledgments

Many people have been invaluable to me in the writing of this book. I am deeply grateful to all of you.

To my Mom and Dad, thank you for making me who I am. My addictions are my own; my best behaviors come from you. You have shaped every positive quality I have. To my brother Daniel, thank you for never letting me rest, for all of your positive reinforcement along the way, and for your wonderful feedback. No one did more than you to help me get this book completed on time. I owe you lots of sushi. To my sister Deborah, thank you for your wisdom and insights when I ventured into your world. Your expertise and ideas have been invaluable. To Scott, thank you for your creativity and enthusiasm and for supporting all of my whacky ideas when this book was still far off on the horizon. To Liliane and Claude, thank you for your endless patience helping with my kids and giving me the time I needed to write.

To Berrett-Koehler, thank you for being the most welcoming, supportive, author-friendly, exciting publisher an author could hope to find. To my editor Johanna Vondeling and my project leader Tiffany Lee, thank you both for believing in me, shepherding me through the process, and providing invaluable insights and support all along the way. It has been an incredible pleasure working with you both. Thank you also to all of the rest of the B-K organization. You made the entire process more enjoyable and stress-free than I ever imagined it could be. To my readers Amelia Borrego, Sharon Jordan-Evans, Andrea Markowitz, Sharon Melnick, and David Shapiro, thank you for your time and your honesty.

To Mike Jaffe, thank you for helping me think through the hardest chapters and always seeing the brightest possibilities. To Karlin Sloan, thank you for writing your book and encouraging and inspiring me to write mine. To Tammy Winnie, thank you for your respect. You helped me build the confidence I needed to see this project through. To Lindsey Pollack, thank you for your guidance in the process of writing a book. This book would never have found a publisher without you.

To Daniel Herrmann, thank you for sharing your struggle with alcoholism and your life-changing experiences with Alcoholics Anonymous. To all the people who have shared with me their encounters with change, thank you for your time and your stories, most notably Ethan Schutz, Emily Golden, Alan Graham, Derek Hanson, and Derrin Hill.

Above all, to my wife Beatrice and my daughters Sophie and Ella, thank you for your laughter and your spirit. Your unwavering support has lifted me up and inspired me through every draft of this book and through everything I do in life.

Understanding Self-Addiction

Questions to get you started:

What is self-addiction?

What are your self-addictions?

Renee calls herself a New Year's Health Nut. In early January she is a regular at the gym, but knows that by February she will have forgotten her New Year's resolution to stay in shape, given up on her exercise crusade, and disappeared from the gym until next year.

Denise is a self-proclaimed "control freak" whose behavior hurts her personal and professional relationships.

Jonathan is an engineer-turned-manager who constantly points out the errors and problems in other people's work. His inability to provide positive feedback is turning his team against him.

What challenge do Renee, Denise, and Jonathan face? They are each addicted to themselves.

What does it mean to be addicted to yourself?

People use the word addiction to describe a variety of behaviors and conditions. There are alcoholics and shopaholics. There are drug addicts and sex addicts. There are compulsive gamblers and compulsive shoplifters. People say they are addicted to food or fitness, chocolate or basketball. But what does it really mean to be addicted to yourself?

There are many different addictions, some of which (alcohol, drugs, gambling, etc.) can destroy people's lives. This book is not meant to be a substitute for treatment of clinical addictions. The addictions I discuss in these pages are behaviors you exhibit on a daily basis. They are your habits and routines. They are the actions you take with your coworkers, your spouse, and your children. They are the behaviors that come out when you are angry or hurt or nervous or unsure of yourself.

These behaviors come out in all areas of life. Someone criticizes you and you turn silent. Perhaps you know that you should try to understand and work to improve, but you are addicted to your silent, cold response. Another time your spouse leaves the kitchen a mess for what seems like the tenth time this week. You may know that yelling about it won't help the situation or your relationship, but you do it anyway. When you go into work you find several co-workers congregated in an office complaining about the new marketing strategy. Maybe you realize that you're only making the situation worse by joining in, but it feels so natural you can hardly help yourself.

Whatever the behaviors are that you wish to change, you may not feel like an addict. You are certainly very talented in many ways and may be an exemplary parent, spouse, leader, and friend. Perhaps you are on the verge of being a perfect ten, if only you quit being so accommodating, paid more attention to your kids, or did a better job of delegating. We all have ways that we can improve ourselves.

Have you ever wondered why self-help is one of the fastest growing industries? Why are there so many books to help people change themselves? Is it that people have so many things that they want to change, or is it that we are simply not very good at changing? At the time of this writing Amazon.com had over 170,000 listings for "diet." Yet, we certainly are not a particularly thin nation. There were over 120,000 items under "leadership." Walk into any corporate executive's office, and you are bound to find a handful, if not dozens, of leadership books. Imagine what work would be like if all of the corporate executives in the country actually practiced half of the leadership skills described in the books they read.

Why don't these leadership and diet books work? Because they provide new behaviors and supply wonderful ideas, but they don't help us address our addictions to our behaviors. We have had our behaviors shaped, molded, and reinforced thousands of times over the course of our lifetimes. We have been conditioned to act in a certain way when faced with certain types of situations. We can't simply come up with something better and turn off the old behavior. It takes time to unlearn the old behavior and to learn to replace it with a new one.

Steven is a learning and development professional who works for a Fortune 500 company. He is also a recovering alcoholic. When I asked him how long it had been since his last drink, he replied, "Every day is a new challenge." He wasn't being vague; he was telling me that it didn't matter how long it had been. The power of the addictive behavior is so strong that if he isn't vigilant every day, it could come back to overwhelm him. Later he shared with me that it had been 17 years since his last drink. Your behavioral addictions may not take a lifetime to overcome. However, the example of alcoholism presents a valuable lesson that a deeply ingrained behavior doesn't change overnight.

The fact remains that you *can* change. Whether you are trying to change something for the first time or you are struggling with something that you have tried to change many times in the past, you can make the change you desire. People have difficulty with change because they don't know *how* to change. They know what they want to do, but they don't know how to adjust when they get into situations that bring out their bad habits. The truth is that you can change if you have an effective plan for how to do so. This book is dedicated to helping you lay out that plan and break your self-addiction.

What are some common self-addictions?

Self-addictions appear in every area of life. You may wish to be a better parent, a better spouse, a better leader, or you may wish to make changes for your own sake, so you can be a better person. In some cases, you may wish to eliminate a behavior that you feel harms you (e.g., controlling behavior). In another situation you may want to begin a new behavior (e.g., regular exercise). Unwanted behaviors may occur in your interactions with others (e.g., yelling at people), or they may occur when you are alone (e.g., criticizing yourself).

Maybe you already have an idea of an area in your life that you wish were different. If not, the checklist on page 5 might help you identify some areas where you'd benefit from change. This exercise is not meant as an opportunity for you to catalogue all the things that you wish to change. Do not get down on yourself if you share many of the behaviors on the list. Instead, focus on those areas you most wish to change now. Also, do not feel restricted by the items listed. Feel free to add your own.

This exercise should start to give you a sense of where some of your self-addictions may lie. Step 1, Identifying Your Self-Addictions, is dedicated to exploring more fully what your self-addictions are and what you most wish to change.

For now, it is important to simply understand that a self-addiction can be any behavior that is used inappropriately. You may even notice that some addictive behaviors are flip sides of the same coin. For example, telling others what to do and doing what you are told can both be self-addictions and illustrate that self-addiction isn't so much about the behavior itself as it is about the inappropriate use of the behavior.

For every addictive behavior listed, you can construct situations in which that behavior makes sense. You can create circumstances in which the behavior is a good and maybe even the best course of ac-

Exercise Identify Self-Addictions		
Identify the three most important behaviors you wish to change now.		
☐ Working too much (or too little)		☐ Speaking before you think
☐ Criticizing others		☐ Thinking too much before you speak
☐ Criticizing yourself		☐ Poor eating habits
☐ Giving too little positive feedback		☐ Being unhappy
☐ Saying "no"		☐ Exercise habits
☐ Controlling others		☐ Spending too little family time
☐ Being defensive		☐ Being pessimistic
☐ Getting angry		☐ Being over-organized
☐ Showing emotion		☐ Needing to be right
☐ Crying		☐ Being helpless
☐ Being silent		☐ Having the last word
☐ Yelling		☐ Being negative
☐ Deferring to others		☐ Telling others what to do
☐ Pushing your opinions on others		☐ Doing what you are told
☐ Being too risk averse		☐ Not listening
☐ Taking too many risks		☐ Other_____

tion. Of course, you can also invent situations where the behaviors would have negative, or even disastrous effects.

Throughout the book we will follow the stories of four individuals who have worked to overcome their self-addictions. Karen, the first individual we will follow, works in customer service for a travel services company. She describes how the very behaviors that served her well in some circumstances were actually self-addictions because of how they hurt her in other situations.

The Pushover

I have always loved making people happy. Luckily, I found a job where I am expected to do just that. When people take vacations with my company, I want those vacations to be perfect. If my customers want a particular dining experience, theater tickets, or a room with a view, I find a way to get it done. People aren't always happy when they come to see me, but I do everything I can to make sure that they leave happy. My job is to take care of people, and I do it pretty well.

I always thought this was a good thing until it sparked troubles for me at home. My husband and daughters have busy lives and lots of needs. I had gotten so good at saying "yes" to people that I didn't even realize how much it had crossed over into my home life. At work I got rewarded for saying "yes." The customers were happy, my boss was happy, and I was happy.

At home I got stuck with the lion's share of the family responsibilities. Every time my daughters needed me or my husband to do something, I was always the one who did it. When it was time for us to decide where to go eat or on vacation, or what color to paint the walls, I never got my choice. One day I realized that I was getting more and more frustrated and resentful toward the people who were most important in my life.

Unfortunately, I had become totally committed to my giving behavior. I don't think anyone intentionally took advantage of me. It was my own fault. For years I had consistently made my needs irrelevant.

Karen's giving behavior had become so ingrained that the situation did nothing to influence her actions. She was unable to identify when she should stick up for her own rights and desires rather than simply accommodate the needs of someone else. This accommodating behavior was a great benefit to her at some times, but a disadvantage at others. So, self-addiction can't be defined by the behavior alone. In order to better understand self-addictions, let's look at where they come from.

Where do addictions come from?

Addictive behaviors serve many purposes, but they all develop through the same four stages:

1. They provide or provided some positive benefit.
2. They become self-reinforcing.

3. They result in negative consequences.

4. You continue to engage in the behavior despite the negative consequences.

Positive Benefit

We become addicted to our own behaviors because at some time, for some reason, we benefited from our actions. Our behavior may have made us feel good about ourselves at some time. It may have boosted our self-esteem and raised our confidence. There are great reasons why our behaviors evolve. They help us to be happier, cope better, improve our performance, decrease our anxiety, or in some way enhance our perception of our lives. These are the reasons the behaviors begin and, if they ended there, they would simply be coping mechanisms, not addictions.

John developed his self-addiction because the behavior made him feel good. Here is how he describes the development of his addictive behavior.

The Talker

I love being around people and making people laugh, but it hasn't always been that way. I was kind of socially inept as a kid. Then I did a class play one year and it was really funny. With someone else writing the words for me I was able to play the part and capture everyone's attention. After that experience, I tried out for every play my school did. It was fantastic. There I was, this kid who no one wanted to talk to normally. But once the curtain went up, it was like I had a room full of friends. I think that the whole experience of theater really built my confidence, and that improved my ability to be social. I started to take the same approach to normal conversations that I had taken on stage —I had to be entertaining.

Getting attention gave John a boost to his self-esteem, which was fine in itself. It became a problem down the line, however, when he needed this attention more and more to simply feel good about himself. That led to problems such as not listening to other people and monopolizing conversations.

There are two ways people benefit from their actions: the actions bring pleasure or take away pain. While John's actions benefited him by making him feel good, other people take action to remove some pain they feel in their lives. Many behaviors are grounded in helping you stop the pain you are feeling. Stopping the hurt can be a very useful action to help you get through difficult times. That's what happened with Susan.

The Worker

I don't think I was a particularly serious student when I got to law school. I made sure to prepare for class, study for tests, and write my papers, but I also made sure to go out and have a good time. There were people in my program who lived in the library, but that certainly wasn't me in the beginning. Then my father was diagnosed with cancer. When he got sick, I simply didn't find things exciting the way I had before. I would go out with my friends and everyone would be having a good time. All I'd be able to think about was how my dad had taken a chemo treatment that day or how he was getting weaker and weaker.

My only escape was studying. I could look through old cases or work in the library at school for hours. I could sit down and study all day without thinking about my father. That may sound callous, but I think it might have been the only thing that kept me sane during that time. My father got sick when I was in the middle of my first year of law school. I ended up finishing at the top of my class because of my father's cancer. I only wish he had been there to see me graduate.

As with John, there was nothing wrong with Susan's behavior when it first developed. It was an effective coping mechanism during a difficult time in her life. It was later that this behavior became problematic, when she used her work to escape from her family and avoid developing deeper relationships with her husband and children.

Self-Reinforcement

Behaviors that outlive their original purpose do so because at some point they become self-reinforcing. When the original purpose or reward for a behavior no longer exists, a new reward can arise from within. This internal reward is strong enough that it can sustain the behavior with or without the original rewards. So even though we may no longer feel the pain and get the praise we once did, those positive associations from our past are enough to reinforce within us that the behavior is good.

Consciously or unconsciously we convince ourselves that the behavior helps us and/or those around us. This pattern persists for long enough that the behavior is cemented in our natural routines. We perform the behavior without even thinking about it. It is our natural response. Even now, it is not an addiction. At this point it is merely a habit, something that is characteristic of who we are. It is only an addiction if we continue to use the behavior in the face of negative consequences.

Negative Consequences

Many behaviors that start out healthy turn unhealthy over time. Sometimes the negative consequences are internal, meaning that we create the consequences for ourselves. These could be physical or psychological and include:

- Stress
- Depression
- Self-criticism
- Self-doubt
- Excessive anger.

Sometimes the negative consequences are external, meaning that they relate to how others react to our behavior. Our behaviors may frustrate, anger, or humiliate those around us. These consequences may affect us in work and/or personal settings and could range from small annoyances to enormous obstacles to our happiness and success. These external consequences could include:

- Poor performance reviews and/or consistently negative feedback at work
- Missing promotion and/or reward opportunities at work
- Shallow and/or unsupportive relationships
- Needless fighting
- Others ending or diminishing once-strong relationships with you.

Let's take another look at John and Susan and some of the consequences they suffered.

The Talker

I remember getting out of a meeting with my team that my manager had decided to attend. I was flying when the meeting ended; I thought it had gone so well. My team was totally united. We came up with some great ideas and everyone seemed to really like the outcomes. Afterwards, my manager called me into his office. I was expecting the best, but the first thing he did was tell me that he was disappointed. He said that during the course of the one-hour meeting he timed my floor time. He said my talking time was over 45 minutes. What's more, he said that I consistently cut off and talked over my team members when they tried to get into the conversation.

Then he got personal. It hurt a lot to hear, but I think this was what forced me to take it seriously. He said, "Look around. Haven't you noticed that you're wearing out your welcome? People don't want to listen to your 20-minute monologues anymore. It's not just with your team, either. Senior managers have talked to me about this. Your peers have talked to me. This is a real problem for you and you need to fix it if you have any hope of being promoted in this organization."

What John heard was upsetting and hurt him personally, but it also helped him considerably to understand the consequences of his actions. When he looked around, he discovered that people who had previously been friendly towards him were always too busy to talk. Discussions would dry up when he arrived. John's behavior was shutting his coworkers out of conversations and alienating him from his own team.

The Worker

You would have thought that my first ulcer at the age of 32 would have been enough to clue me into the fact that I had created a less-than-healthy lifestyle for myself. In fact, it didn't even faze me. It was just one more illness in a long list that I had to deal with. It seemed that I was always sick: colds, flu, coughs. I figured if they weren't keeping me from doing what I always did, which was go to work, then they probably were nothing to worry about. No, I didn't figure things out for almost 15 more years.

Somehow, a couple of years after my father's death, I managed to break away from work long enough to meet someone and get married. I even had 2 kids, though I worked through both pregnancies, right up until the delivery. Then, about a year ago, my sister had a dinner party at her house. I wasn't being very good company. My mind was on a project that would be starting soon at work. I picked up a photo album so I could pretend that my mind was focused on something at least in the vicinity of the party.

At first it was nice. There was a picture of my sister and her husband with their kids and my son. I remembered they had taken him to a professional basketball game a while ago. Then I found another one of them with my kids at what looked like a barbecue at a park. I had always appreciated how close our families were and how much my kids really seemed to bond with my sister's family. The further I went in her photo album, the more I came across pictures of my kids with her family. I picked up another album and discovered the same thing.

It was one of the saddest things I had ever experienced. As I looked through my sister's photo albums, I realized how much of my kids' lives she had experienced and how little I had. The most frightening part of this experience was that in the middle of this epiphany, I

was still thinking about work. I still had that project bouncing around in
my head. That was the moment for me. That was when I realized that
I had to change.

While John was hurting himself at work, Susan was hurting herself
at home. She was pushing her own kids out of her life. Your own
behaviors and their consequences may not be as apparent to you
now. However, we all engage in behaviors that result in negative
consequences. These consequences may be small at first, but over
time may grow into significant issues if not addressed. Just think
about what your spouse, child, coworker, sibling, or parent would
say if asked what they would like to change about you.

Continued Behavior

Continuing the behaviors that harm us is the most telling characteristic of self-addiction. We are an intelligent species. You'd think that
we'd know enough to not do things that hurt us. Here then is the
key characteristic of self-addiction: despite negative consequences
for our actions, we continue to engage in the same behaviors. Why
do we do this to ourselves? I asked myself this question regularly in
the first couple of years of my marriage. Here is a typical dialogue
that my wife and I would have:

> [My wife and I are in the car. I'm driving.]
> Wife: Do you know that you have to make a left soon?
> Me: I know. [said with a mildly annoyed tone of voice]
> Wife: Why don't you get into the left lane?
> Me: Well, it's a good thing I have you to navigate for me.
>   [dripping with sarcasm]
> Wife: What is your problem? [said with more than mild an-
>   noyance]

It was typically around this point in the conversation that I
would realize that I was in trouble. A reasonable person would rec-

ognize the folly of fighting this fight. If I had even a shred of control over myself during these conversations, I wouldn't have continued them. Yet, my addiction to defensiveness would push me to respond.

> Me: What exactly do you think happens to me when I'm alone in the car? Do you think that I drive around permanently lost and getting into accidents every three miles?

Now that felt good when I said it, but as an outside observer, you can probably guess that the good feeling didn't last long. My wife got angrier and, as a result, I became more miserable. Neither her anger nor my misery was surprising when it occurred. I knew what my actions would create. After all, I had played out similar scenes many times before. I was so addicted to my defensiveness that I continued to engage in the behavior despite the negative consequences that it created for me and for my wife.

Albert Einstein defined insanity as "doing the same thing over and over again and expecting different results." Similarly, you could say that the definition of self-addiction is doing the same thing over and over again, knowing you'll get the same bad results.

Thankfully, I believe I am a recovering defensive-behavior addict. Like Steven, who despite 17 years without a drink considers each day a new challenge, I know that I need to remain vigilant, aware, and in control in order to keep these behaviors from creeping back into my life. Even if I could permanently eliminate all defensive behavior, there are plenty of other changes I'd like to make to myself. Each time I feel as though I'm on steady ground with one self-addiction, I recognize another that I'd like to change.

That is the nature of personal development. It is a lifelong pursuit. This book gives you the tools to develop and change yourself into the person you want to be. Of course, if you are going to take on this challenge, there should be some real rewards.

What do you have to gain?

Imagine if you became expert in adapting your behaviors. Think what it would be like if each time you said to yourself, "I wish I were better at that," or "I wish I didn't do that all the time," you had an effective method to change your behavior. Developing the skill to make those changes consistently and effectively would change your whole life.

Alcoholics Anonymous recommends three specific changes to prospective members:

1. Stop drinking.
2. Go to meetings.
3. Change your whole life.

Hopefully, you are not battling anything as challenging as addiction to alcohol and do not, therefore, have so great a depth from which to climb. In fact, you probably feel great about yourself and your life. Even so, you can still change your whole life and make it better than it already is. Personal development isn't an item on a to-do list that you can check off once it's complete. It is a lifelong endeavor to help you be your best self and live your best life.

This book offers a system to help you do three things:

1. Identify important changes that you would like to make.
2. Make those changes.
3. Sustain them over time.

Whether you are seeking ways to improve on a great situation or feel that your life is far from what you desire, your own behaviors play a critical role. Breaking your self-addictions and putting in place new, healthy behaviors will affect you profoundly at home and work, with family and friends. It will make you a better parent, spouse, worker, and leader. Breaking your self-addictions truly has the potential to change your whole life.

How are self-addictions broken?

The process for breaking self-addictions will take effort. There are diet books that trumpet "easy weight loss" and relationship books that talk of "easy marriage." For every development topic there is an author who has written about an "easy" path. In reality there is no easy marriage, parenting, weight loss, or leadership. These all take hard work, effort, and dedication, and rarely are these changes permanent. Steven, the recovering alcoholic from earlier in this chapter, hasn't had a drink in 17 years, but every day is still a new challenge for him. Change doesn't happen overnight. That's why the method for breaking your self-addictions may be simple, but it is not easy. That doesn't mean you can't do it. It just takes effort and a targeted plan for you to be surprisingly effective at changing your behaviors.

The challenge is this: addictions have a strong and powerful hold on you. In order to break them, you need to be even stronger. Unfortunately, your addictions aren't just inside of you, they are all around you. Your behaviors result from a combination of who you are and how your surroundings push you to act. Over your lifetime you have tuned yourself to be extremely sensitive to any cues that push you toward your addictive behaviors. At the same time, you have suppressed or eliminated the cues that push you toward more beneficial behaviors.

In order to overcome this imbalance, you need to create an environment in and around you that cues your new behaviors. You need to surround yourself with an environment that rarely lets you forget about the change you are trying to make. You need to make it so that the cues for your new behaviors are regularly, if not always, in front of you. Only then will you have the strength to force yourself to continue to confront the addiction until you have truly broken it.

This book helps you develop that strength as you raise your awareness, build support around you, and take consistent actions. These are the three circles that make up the Circles of Strength model for change and make it possible to break self-addictions. All around

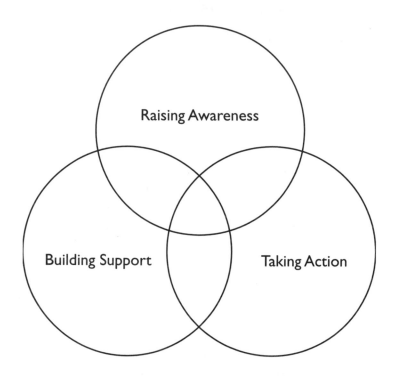

Circles of Strength

you there are cues that support your behavior or at least elements in your environment that allow your behavior to continue. You are surrounded by things that enable your self-addiction. When you build your Circles of Strength, you recreate yourself and your surroundings to support your new behavior and break the self-addiction.

Each of the next three sections of this book, Raising Awareness, Building Support, and Taking Action, will describe one of the Circles of Strength, and each section will contain three steps to build that circle. You will go through nine total steps to help you break your self-addictions, make the changes you want in your life, and become the person you want to be.

What if you face a clinical addiction?

Alcohol, drugs, and gambling are just a few of the clinical addictions for which there are highly effective treatment programs. If you face a clinical addiction, this book may be a useful supplement to a course of treatment. However, it is in no way a substitute for professional help. If these are the addictions you face, I encourage you to get help far beyond what I offer here. For more information on treatment programs for these and other addictions, please see "Help For Clinical Addictions" in the back of this book.

Part I

Raising Awareness

In this section, you create a Circle of Awareness to increase the information and knowledge you have of your self-addiction. The Circle of Awareness forms the foundation of your efforts to change. You may have already identified specific behaviors you would like to change, or you might need help figuring out what those behaviors are. Whatever your situation, it will be valuable for you to take steps to raise your awareness of not only what your addictions are, but how they affect you and those around you and what commitments you need to make to see the process through to completion. You will go through three steps to raise your awareness and surround yourself with the information you need to break your self-addictions.

Step 1 Identify Your Self-Addictions
Identify your self-addictions and select the one
you most want to work on now.

Step 2 Realize the Consequences
Increase your understanding of your own actions and their impact
by looking at the outcomes of your actions.

Step 3 Make Meaningful Commitments
Make meaningful acknowledgments of your self-
addictions and powerful commitments to realize the changes you
wish to make.

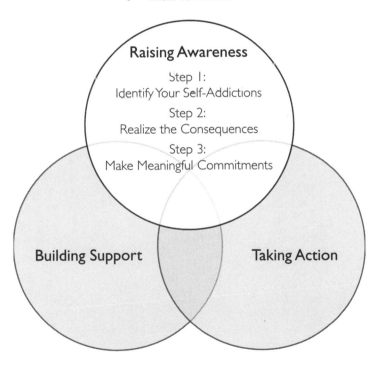

Circles of Strength

Identify Your Self-Addictions

Questions to get you started.

What are the behaviors that get you in trouble?

What are your key self-addictions?

I recently started working with two new clients. The first, Nicholas, was very excited about the coaching opportunity. He knew that coaching was in vogue and it made him feel cool. However, he had no real idea of how he wanted to use the opportunity. In fact, Nicholas struggled at the beginning of our work. I asked him a lot of questions and got lots of silence in return. It took a few sessions for him to figure out his goals for the coaching. Nicholas faced the formidable challenge of discovering the changes he wanted to make, personally and professionally.

The second client, Carmen, knew exactly what she wanted to do with our coaching time. She told me that she was completely preoccupied with how other people viewed her. At home she was constantly trying to keep up with the Joneses and maintain an image of perfection. At work she ingratiated herself to everyone and was incapable of taking any risks for fear of making a mistake and looking bad. She was ready from the first moment we sat down to charge into these challenges.

If you are like Nicholas, this chapter will help you to think through your opportunities for change and identify what you wish to work on for the remainder of this book. If you are like Carmen, this chapter will give you a chance to reflect on your change and ensure that you are on the right track. Even if you think you know exactly what you need to change, it is possible that you have missed the mark on what behavior would really be most beneficial for you to develop. What you think is important for you to change may be exactly on track, or it might be minor compared with other issues you face.

Whether you are reading this book because you know what you want to change or just because it seems interesting to you, this chapter will help you identify your core self-addictions that you will work on throughout the rest of the book.

How can you discover your self-addictions?

It's now time to identify the behaviors that you most wish to change. What are your self-addictions? What are the behaviors that have been so difficult to change in the past? What behaviors have hurt you at work? What do you do that gets you into trouble with your spouse? What do you do that frustrates you and leaves you kicking yourself for days? Perhaps you kick yourself too much and that is the addiction you wish to break. Whatever your addictions, now is the time to identify them and take the first steps towards changing.

There are three methods we will explore for becoming aware of your addictions:

- Contrasting with others
- Getting shocked
- Asking around.

Let's look at each of these in turn.

Contrasting With Others

Contrasting with others is simply recognizing some of the positive and admirable qualities in those around you and realizing that you would like to emulate them. That is what happened with me and my wife, Beatrice, when we first met. Beatrice opened my eyes to my own behavior because her behavior was so contrary to mine. We had been dating for only three or four weeks and were watching a baseball game in her living room. Ken Griffey, Jr. was up to bat and Beatrice was trying to impress me with her baseball knowledge. She said to me, "His father played baseball, too, didn't he?" She was referring to Ken Griffey, Jr.'s father who had indeed played professional baseball. At that point, I was duly impressed with her knowledge and was about to say just that. Before I had time to comment to that effect, she added, "What was his father's name?"

I looked at her with some surprise, and I said, "You want to know what Ken Griffey, *Junior's* father's name was?" She returned a blank stare. "That would be Ken Griffey, *Senior.*" Beatrice finally understood her error. What happened next was one of the most amazing things I have ever seen. She laughed. Not a chuckle or a short, embarrassed "silly me" kind of laugh, but a full-on, when-is-it-going-to-end, tears-running-down-her-face, please-make-it-stop-because-my-belly-hurts kind of laugh.

I don't think I had ever seen someone appear more comfortable with themselves or have more self-confidence than she seemed to have in that moment. She had no fear that I would think she was dumb, and why would I? I knew that she was extremely intelligent. None of that would have mattered to me if our roles had been reversed.

Had I made this same mistake, I would have constructed elaborate excuses. I would have told detailed stories about baseball and myself to convince her and everyone else that I wasn't stupid. I would have gotten angry at myself and beaten myself up for several days over it. I might have avoided seeing her for a few days just so that the mistake would become old news. All of this would have done little to erase the mistake and much to make me look even more foolish than did the original comment.

It wasn't until I really got to see my wife laugh at herself that I realized I was missing out on something. It was only through knowing her that I was able to understand and admit to myself that I was addicted to my own feelings of intellectual pride. I was addicted to the feeling I got from believing that others thought I was intelligent.

My need to be right and to look intelligent affected me in many ways beyond simply limiting my laughter. That I couldn't laugh at myself only made my own errors embarrassing for everyone present. Worse though was what my need to be perceived as intelligent did to me at work. In my first job, I rushed to provide the answers, to show that I was smart, sometimes shutting out my peers in the process. In my first managerial position I spent most of my time telling and very little time asking questions. This behavior made me feel good because it helped me to believe that my wisdom was useful and appreciated. However, it hurt my team members by minimizing their opportunities to provide input and develop their own solutions.

I had a problem and seeing my wife's carefree nature, self-confidence, and eagerness to laugh was the contrast I needed in order to recognize, understand, and admit to my self-addiction. Her comment about Ken Griffey, Jr. gave me the "Aha!" moment I needed to begin the exploration and see various other ways that this self-addiction was hurting me.

Contrast can best be described as seeing someone do something well, and having the flash of insight that this is something which you would like to improve in yourself. You contrast another person's ability with your own, and the contrast provides the inspiration. After that, it is up to you to continue with the necessary exploration to understand and admit to the addiction.

How do you find this inspiration? Inspiration is something that is just supposed to happen. It comes to you in a flash. In the movie *Back to the Future*, Christopher Lloyd's character was installing a new shower head. He slipped and banged his head on the side of the bathtub. When he awoke, he had a picture in his mind of the flux capacitor, the device that made time travel possible. He was inspired by a mild concussion. Another famous, albeit mythical, knock on the head was Sir Isaac Newton's. While sitting under the apple tree an apple fell and knocked him on the head. Voila! Gravity was discovered.

So what do you do if you don't have the good fortune of being knocked on the head? I was lucky enough to be inspired by someone close to me. What if no one has stepped into your life to provide similar inspiration? The answer is probably that they have, but you just haven't realized it yet. You absolutely can manufacture your own inspiration. You merely need to ask yourself the right questions.

Who are the people whose actions motivate you, surprise you, impress you, or leave you on an emotional high? These people could be your friends, family members, and coworkers. You should consider the people you look up to, the ones you most admire. They could be people you know or public figures. They can be gurus in the field of leadership or fitness or parenting or marriage. They can be living or dead. The first step is simply to identify who these people are.

In order to identify the contrast, you need to recognize the behaviors you admire in them and then be truthful about your own behaviors in that realm. Consider the following examples.

Person I Admire	His/Her Behaviors	My Related Behaviors
Family—Eileen	Shows endless patience when people around her are slow to understand	Show frustration and annoyance toward others
Friends—Jeff	Dedicates self to necessary actions no matter how much he dislikes them	Procrastinate undesirable tasks and perform them casually
Coworkers—Kara	Takes risks and dreams big	Same
Gurus—Jack Welch	Is incredibly direct, honest, and fair in dealing with star and problem employees	Avoid directly confronting problematic behavior
Public Figures— Roger Clemens (pro baseball player)	Pushes himself and works relentlessly during off-season to come back strong every year	Slow down considerably during nonpeak work times

You may find that some of the contrasts are more important than others. For example, if this chart were yours, you might decide that the contrast with Eileen is deeply important to you and something you want to change. However, although you admire Roger Clemens's work ethic, you may not wish to emulate it. Perhaps you are completely at ease with your work style but still find his impressive. That's a perfectly acceptable and valuable outcome from this process.

> **Special Note:** Starting with this exercise and throughout the rest of the book, it will be valuable for you to record your notes from the exercises in a single place so that you can easily review what you have done and see your progress along the way. I recommend that you keep a notebook specifically for this purpose.

Exercise 1.1   Find Contrast

Construct your own chart like the one on page 25. For each person who inspires, impresses, or surprises you, identify their behaviors and character traits that you most admire. Focus on things that they do or say or their demeanor, rather than characteristics of their fame, fortune, or position. It may help to ask yourself the following questions:

- How do I feel when I see him/her? Why?
- What does s/he do that gives me a feeling of awe?

For each characteristic that you identified in someone else, describe your own behavior in that area and specify how you are similar and/or different. Next, make a list of those behaviors you wish to emulate.

From this exercise you will begin to see similarities and differences between you and the people you admire. You will begin to see behaviors that you may wish to change. Later in this chapter we will look further at these behaviors and determine which one you want to work on as you read the rest of this book. First, let's look at our next method of identifying self-addictions: getting shocked.

Getting Shocked

As with contrast, shock comes from an interaction with another person, but in a very different context. You get shocked when someone tells you that you are doing something that isn't working. These shocks can be direct and specific, or they can be vague. Either way, the underlying characteristic is that someone sends you a message that your behavior needs adjustment. Darrell, a marketing executive for a retail clothing company, was shocked into an understanding of his addictions. Here is his story.

The Critic

I was surrounded by greatness, at home by my kids and at work by my team members. They were all interesting, fun, talented people. My kids' teachers told me how great they were. My boss and my colleagues raved about the people who worked for me. I had every reason to be happy with the people around me. Then, in less than a month, I got three wake-up calls, three painful wake-up calls.

I was in my office early when Alexis, my top performer, came to see me. She had been with me for a little over a year and had impressed everyone from the start. I thought she had a bright future in the company, but she came in that morning to give me her resignation. I was completely taken aback and told her as much. I told her I thought she was very talented and destined for senior roles in our company and she shouldn't leave since she had such a bright future here. Then the real shock came. She told me that this was the first time I had ever given her the impression that she wasn't completely incompetent. That was tough to take. So tough, in fact, that I blew it off.

Three weeks later I had an incident with my oldest son, Nate. It was report card time, and he had done pretty well. He had mostly A's with one B and a C in History. I didn't even think about it. I just dove right in and started asking him questions all about the C. How did that happen? How much was he studying? What was he going to do to bring the grade up? I guess I was pretty stern with him in the way I asked the questions, but he certainly got me back with my last question.

"Why didn't we know about his difficulties before report card time?" I said "we" meaning me and his mother. He told me that his mom did know. He asked her not to say anything to me because I always rip into him on the smallest things. Then he yelled at me. My son never yells at me, but he did then. I was so shocked I don't remember exactly what he said, but I remember the basic message: "What's the point? Why should I try when nothing is ever good enough?"

Less than a week after that, one of my other top performers, Evan, came to give me his resignation. At first I thought that Alexis had taken him along with her, but the timing was just a coincidence. Evan had also been dissatisfied and had looked for and found a new job. When I asked him why he wanted to leave he talked about the opportunities in the new job, but I could tell he was holding back. So I asked him point blank, "Are you leaving because of me?" He still said no, but it didn't sound like there was a lot of conviction.

Then I asked him if I was tough to work for. That finally got him to open up. He told me that I made things tough at times. He said that I always saw the flaws. I always pointed out errors. I publicly ripped people's ideas apart and I never lifted people up. I never praised anyone. I never made people feel great about me as their leader or about themselves and their work.

All I wanted to do was to tell him he didn't know what he was talking about, except that he did know and so did my son and so did Alexis. I realized then that everyone else on my team and in my family probably knew as well. All this time I had been taking the people I respected and cared about most in the world and making them feel bad about themselves. I'd like to think that one wake-up call would have been enough, but three made it impossible for me to ignore.

When a shock comes to us naturally, it is like a bucket of ice water thrown in our face. Darrell's experiences opened his eyes to a behavior that he didn't even realize was there. Sometimes shocks come in exactly that fashion—comments from a respected source directly pointing out the addiction at play. These shocks hit us in such a way that we cannot ignore them.

Other times, the messages are not so direct. The source is not as trusted. Often we turn away these shocks that could do so much to help us if we were only receptive. We are able to do this because we are all endowed with natural shock absorbers.

Our shock absorbers are our defense mechanisms. They come in various guises, but they all serve to do the same thing, to diminish the impact of a shock to the system. Since shocks generally come as a realization that we are engaging in undesirable behaviors, our shock absorbers do their best to convince us that the situation isn't so bad, or that the fault lies elsewhere. Consider how often you've said any of the following things to yourself when confronted with your own undesirable behavior:

- Oh, she doesn't know what she's talking about.

- He's criticizing me? He should take a look in the mirror.

- I could stop this any time I wanted.

- Why is he making this into such a big deal? It's nothing.

Our defenses are set up to convince us we are in control, are good, and our behavior is justified. While this may all be true, the possibility remains that, good as we are and justified as our behaviors may be, they still may not be healthy for us. Our systems may need the shock.

Recognizing Shocks

In order to recognize shocks, you need to become open to your own imperfection. That may sound crazy. We should *all* be able to admit that we're not perfect. The challenge is being receptive when someone else says you're not perfect or when your emotions are running high. Whether or not it's warranted, when people receive criticism they frequently perceive it as an attack. Of course, sometimes it is, but that doesn't mean there isn't truth to it. At these times, you may go on the counterattack, become silent, or you may feign acceptance. Whatever your response is in the moment, you can benefit from examining the criticism, whether constructive or malicious, and taking from it the kernel of truth that makes it useful.

The first step is to recognize the various ways that the shock can be delivered. Darrell's situation was easy. Trusted colleagues and family members walked right up to him and said, "Darrell, you are too critical." Unfortunately, every message isn't so obvious. While a shock can come from someone directly criticizing you or your behavior, it can also become apparent from the following:

- Someone avoids speaking with or seeing you.

- Someone gets frustrated with you.

- You get frustrated with yourself or beat yourself up over something you did.

- You get annoyed with someone else.

- You are ashamed of yourself.

- You get into a fight.

- You find yourself doing things or spending time with people you previously found distasteful or contemptible.

I'm not saying that every time someone criticizes you or you get into an argument that it is an indication of a self-addiction. However, these are good events to examine when trying to identify shocks. There are many different situations that can result in a shock to your system. The next exercise will help you recognize shocks you may have missed in the past and open you up to feeling new shocks in the future.

When looking for the shocks in your life, you are seeking the places where (once you recognize your own behavior) what you find surprises you. By its very nature, a shock is harder than a contrast for you to uncover on your own. The contrast you can discover by comparing yourself with people whom you admire. The shock can only be exposed by comparing your true self with the image of yourself you hold.

How do you know when your true self is at odds with your image of yourself? Usually your emotions flare up. They are trying to protect you from discovering that you are not who you think you are. You are not the person you want to be. These may be times in your life when you are angry, frustrated, sad, ashamed, envious, furious, embarrassed, or aggravated. When are you critical of yourself or others? When are you downright mean? When are you at your worst?

Exercise 1.2   Shock Yourself
Identify the situations in your life that most frequently bring out negative emotions or bring out the strongest negative emotions, then answer the following questions: • What happened that caused me to act the way I did? • What specific behaviors did I exhibit? • What would I like to do differently when faced with similar situations in the future? From your answers to these questions, identify any behaviors that you would like to change. Add them to your list from the Find Contrast exercise found earlier in this chapter.

If at this point your list of behaviors to change looks long to you, don't feel bad. Anyone who is honest during these exercises will admit to having flaws. It doesn't make you a bad person. In fact, recognizing that you aren't perfect and working to improve yourself makes you a great person. Whether your list is long or short, if you are unsure of what change will be most beneficial for you, there is one more excellent way for you to identify your own self-addictions.

Asking Around

If you've read this far, it is clear that you truly want to improve something about yourself. However, it isn't always easy to identify what change you want to make. Even when you do identify a possible change, how do you know that what you've selected is actually the best place to put your efforts? Many people struggle to identify the most important changes they could make in themselves and/or their lives. Sometimes people mistakenly select a change that isn't really important. Bringing other people in at this point in the process can help you to clarify what the important changes are for you and will get you started on the right path.

Do you ever look at the people in your life, your coworkers, friends, significant other or family members, and wonder why they do the things they do? Why is he so careless? Why does she beat herself up that way? Why is he so condescending? Why is she so angry all the time? Maybe you don't wonder why; rather, you simply wish your boss would be more supportive, your friend more positive, or your spouse more willing to stand up for herself. Most people do wonder about and wish for these kinds of things. This simply means that somewhere in your life, other people have probably had these same kinds of thoughts about you. Imagine if you asked the important people in your life the following questions:

- What do you really appreciate about me as a spouse/ parent/manager/worker/friend/son/daughter?

- How can I be a better spouse/parent/manager/worker/ friend/son/daughter?

These are simple questions, but they can have a great deal of power. You may learn something new. You may have to face something that you didn't want to admit to yourself. You may discover wonderful truths about yourself and how others perceive you. You may find the answer to what you truly want to work on through the rest of this process (Exercise 1.3).

You also may not get any meaningful answers the first time that you ask. These are unusual questions for people to hear. They

---

Exercise 1.3   Ask Around

Ask the important people in your life the following questions:

- What do you really appreciate about me as a spouse/parent/manager/ worker/friend/son/daughter?

- How can I be a better spouse/parent/manager/worker/friend/son/ daughter?

If you don't get a clear answer to either of these questions, tell the person to give it some thought and then ask again in a few days. From the answers you receive, identify any behaviors that you would like to change. Add them to your list from the other exercises found earlier in this chapter.

may be surprised by them. They may not really understand what you are asking or they may be uncertain about how to respond. As powerful as I think these questions are, I think they grow in power the second time you ask them. When you ask someone how you can be better, they may say they don't know or that you are wonderful the way you are. Don't let them off the hook. Tell them that you will come back in a few days to ask again. That will tell them that you are serious about the question and truly want their input.

It is extremely important at this point that you *don't panic*. You may see a lot of changes you would like to make. That's okay. Everyone who is truly self-aware should be able to build a list of behaviors they would like to change. You don't have to try to change everything at once, nor should you. For now, just be aware that there are changes you would like to make.

Levels of Awareness

This chapter helped you build awareness of yourself. It helped you to uncover and recognize those behaviors that might be holding you back. When you turn your attention to the changes you want to make, it is important to make choices so that the changes do not overwhelm you. Trying to undertake too many changes can create frustration and lead to the loss of all of the changes. For that reason, before you continue on to the next chapter, follow Exercise 1.4 to choose your course of action.

Exercise 1.4   Select a Self-Addiction

As a result of the exercises in this chapter, you've listed many behaviors you may wish to change. It's time for you to review the list and ask yourself the following questions:

- How does each behavior affect me now?
- How will each behavior affect me in the future?
- Which behavior change would have the greatest impact on my life?

Select just one behavior you wish to change. That will form the basis for your work throughout the rest of this book.

There is no formula for determining what is most important for you to change. Only you can ultimately decide what change is worth your time and effort. In the end, whatever you decide to change, that is the best choice for you at that moment. You are the one who has to be motivated for this work, so your decision is what's best for you. If you have made this choice, you have reached your first major milestone in the process. You're ready to take your next step and realize the consequences.

Realize the Consequences

Questions to get you started:

How well do you know yourself?

Who knows you better than you
know yourself?

"I don't have the foggiest idea," my client said to me. He had just finished telling me about a fabulously kindhearted and helpful thing
he had done for one of his employees. I then asked him, "How do
your actions look to her?" I asked this because his wonderful action
was met by his employee with anger and resentment. When he told
me he didn't "have the foggiest idea," it was clear that he saw his actions only through the lens of his own intentions.

All he had done was ask one of his star associates for progress
reports on work that she was doing for one of their clients. He knew
it was an important client. He wanted to offer input. He wanted to
make his broad experience available to improve the quality of the
service to the client. He wanted to be helpful. He didn't want to
be a burden, stifle creativity, question anyone's capability, or micro-
manage. He saw his action only in the best possible light.

That's how most of us see our actions. We naturally evaluate ourselves according to our best intentions. We see our best actions as a
reflection of who we are and our worst actions as necessities brought
on by the circumstances we faced. Even when we try to be critical of
our own actions, it is hard to realize how differently we appear to
others. Of course, when others view us, no matter what the circumstances, they will usually judge us according to our actions. And they
will generally be far more creative than we are in identifying all of the
unsavory motives that could have led us to our actions.

How can you increase your motivation to change?

In this chapter you will raise your awareness to a new level by realizing the consequences of your actions. Identifying the behavior we
want to change is where many of us stop building our awareness. We
think that change comes from knowing what to change and acting
on that knowledge. In fact, this is the shallowest level of awareness.
It keeps our awareness focused solely on ourselves and our perceptions of our behaviors. Attempts to change based on this level of
awareness are like attempts to swim based on dipping your toes in
a freezing swimming pool. It is all too easy once we've felt the frigid
water to convince ourselves that we didn't really want to swim. Like-
wise, we can convince ourselves that the change isn't worth it or that
it couldn't possibly be successful anyway. Real awareness and real
change frequently require much deeper exploration.

To continue to build your Circle of Awareness, you will look
at various ways your self-addiction affects your happiness and personal success. Seeing how your current actions cause negative results and how different actions could create a more positive future
will increase your motivation for the work ahead. You will surround
yourself with information by bringing into your awareness the perspectives of people who are around you all the time. You will see
not just your past actions, but how changing your behavior could
affect your present and future as well. Specifically, you will look at
the consequences of your change in the following areas:

  •   Family, friends, and colleagues

- Past, present, and future
- Possibilities of success.

There is no easy way to determine that one amount of awareness is insufficient and another is adequate to the task of change. However, the more challenging a change, the more awareness you need. This chapter is the bridge between knowing what you want to change and being ready to make commitments to that change. In order to be ready to make those commitments, you have to be absolutely convinced that the outcomes of the change are worth the struggle. That conviction comes from realizing the consequences of your actions.

Family, Friends, and Colleagues

As you seek to add to the information that will support your change efforts, one key place to look is the people with whom you interact. Almost everything you do has an effect on the people around you. Understanding this can play an important motivational part in supporting your change. You may give up on a change when it is only you who will be hurt or let down by the failure. However, when you recognize that others will also be hurt, you will be more likely to maintain your effort.

Let's take another look at Susan, the workaholic lawyer. Here is how she described her experience.

The Worker

It was obvious to me, really. I worked a lot. When I wasn't working, I was thinking about work. I knew it would be great if I spent more time with my family. I'd made New Year's resolutions to do that for several years. I'd make sure we had a couple of family dinners during January. Maybe we would go skiing for a weekend. Then I was back to my old routine and I'd see my husband and kids in passing a couple of times a week.

When I saw my sister's photo albums and realized that I wasn't there for a lot of my own family's family events, I felt a piercing sadness. I thought that would be the catalyst. That would be the push that finally got me to change my ways. Yet one month after seeing those pictures I was back working as hard as ever.

Fortunately, this time I really wanted things to be different. When I realized that I was back to my old routine, I went to speak with my husband about it. I had shared my resolutions with him before, told him all the things I wanted to change, and explained how I was going to be a better wife and mom. This time I tried something different.

Instead of telling him, I asked him. I put him on the witness stand and put my lawyer skills to good use. I asked him what it was like for him to be married to someone who works so much. I grilled him on what our kids thought of me and my work. I got him to tell me how my work had hampered his life and his hopes for the future. Finally, I worked with him and together we formulated a picture of what life could be like for our family going forward.

It was an exhausting, sometimes painful, and sometimes joyful conversation. It was also one of our best talks in years. When we were through, I saw my situation in a whole new light. I was no longer looking at the change from my own perspective. I was seeing myself through the eyes of my family. I saw the good and the bad. Perhaps most importantly, I saw how life could be different for all of us in the future if I made the changes that had eluded me in the past.

Susan gained the perspective of how her actions felt to her husband and his views on how they affected her kids. Her conversation with her husband exposed how her current behavior affected her whole family and it revealed how her own and her family's lives could change for the better. She gained the perspective of the impact of her actions on others.

She had thought of many reasons for changing her work habits: health, work-life balance, fun and happiness, etc. In the end, what got her to view the change differently and make the necessary effort was the impact of her habits on her husband and kids. She had wanted to change before, but when she really understood the situation from her family's perspective, the change took on a whole new meaning.

This information was valuable and motivated Susan to change because the relationship was important. As you seek to gain perspective from other people, it is important to remember that the reason for collecting this information is to feed your motivation for the change. For this reason, the people you consider should be the people you care about. It will do you much less good to realize that your impatience annoys the checkout person at the store than it will to realize that it angers your wife and kids and causes them to withdraw from spending time with you.

You can see how others view you in two ways:

- Imagine their perspective
- Ask for their perspective.

Imagining How Others see You

Think about times that you have exhibited the behavior you want to change. Try to imagine the situation from the perspective of the people around you. Don't picture the scene from your eyes or even from a fly-on–the-wall viewpoint. Get inside the head of the person with whom you are interacting. See yourself engaging in the behavior. Watch yourself through his eyes. Describe yourself as he would describe you. Imagine his internal response to you. What does he think about as he observes you? How does your behavior affect her opinion of you? Now remember her external response. What did she do when you exhibited the behavior? What more do you think she wanted to do?

Exercise 2.1   See Yourself

Identify how your behaviors affect different people in your life by answering the questions below. Be sure to consider how these questions apply to family, friends, and coworkers.

- How do my actions make them feel?
- What do they think of me and my behavior?
- How do my actions make them act?

Asking How Others See You

Once you have recorded your thoughts, there is a second step that you can take to more fully understand others' perspectives. Just as Susan, The Worker, did, you can interview people to seek their direct input on how your behavior affects them. Approaching people in this way is a big step and not one to be taken lightly. It implies a commitment to change and an acknowledgement that you are aware that your behaviors hurt others. At the same time, it can be a powerful catalyst to move you forward in your change effort.

When you are ready to ask people for their perspectives, select those whose opinions you respect and whose integrity you trust. If you are afraid that the person will use the conversation against you, don't speak with them. These discussions should only be held with people you truly feel can be relied upon to be honest with you during the conversation and respectful of the information after the conversation.

While they should act responsibly regarding how they treat the discussion, you should be respectful regarding how you handle their honesty. Listen to what they have to say and resist the temptation to defend yourself or your actions. Otherwise, you are sure to stop their candor. Besides, there is nothing to defend. However they saw the situation was their perspective, and that is exactly what you are looking to discover.

On the next page is a script that you can follow during your interviews. It is only a guide. Feel free to ask additional questions as you see fit. Just remember that your primary goal is to understand how other people experience you and your behavior, not to defend yourself or help them see things from your perspective. The best thing that you can do is ask questions—and then just be silent and take in the responses.

When you conduct these conversations, write down the points that made you feel *least* comfortable. Those will be the ones that are most likely to keep you motivated as you move forward in the process.

One possible outcome from these conversations is that you will hear from others that your behavior isn't a big deal to them or

---

Interview Script

[Name], I have something I'd like to discuss with you and I'd really appreciate your honesty and candor. You see, there is something in myself that I'd like to change, and I'm trying to understand it from the perspective of the important people in my life, people like you. I'd really like your help. I realize that I [state the behavior you wish to change].

- Have you noticed that I do that?

- How does it affect you when I do that?

- How does it make you feel?

- What do you wish I would do instead?

Thank you so much for your input. I really appreciate your honesty.

---

doesn't really affect them. They may say that they never noticed it or don't think you do it. These answers raise some questions for you. Is this really a behavior that you need to change? Have you mistaken a harmless habit for a self-addiction?

These are tough questions that only you can answer for yourself. However, as you seek to answer them, keep one more question in mind: Are they being dishonest to spare your feelings or to avoid their own discomfort at telling you the truth? People are frequently reluctant to provide honest feedback on other people's shortcomings. Not everyone will feel comfortable sharing their opinions and experiences of your behaviors. In the end, you have to be the judge of just how your behavior affects you and those around you.

Past, Present, and Future Impact

Your behaviors can affect you in a number of ways and can influence different areas of your life at various times. Sometimes these effects may all be negative. For example, weight problems might hurt your self-esteem and happiness early in life, your relationships and career later on, and finally your health. Other times they may be mixed, as was the case for Karen, The Pushover.

The Pushover

I remember so many times being in positions where I had opportunities to help and take care of people. In college I remember always taking on the positions that no one else wanted. I was always willing to be the secretary of the club or to volunteer for a fundraising drive. I saw my friends turn away when people asked them for help, but I was never able to do that. I always felt like I didn't have a choice.

Then, when I started working it was the same thing. I worked in retail clothing stores and as a waitress where I was always looking out for my customers' needs. I had to make everyone happy. Then I got my current job, where I'm expected to make everyone's vacation experience the best it can possibly be. I've heard my group referred to as the Stepford Wives, because we try to make everything so perfect. I like to think of us as simply applying a different standard in order to keep people happy.

Up until recently that's been fine, but a couple of months ago I was promoted to a management position. I've seen managers who try to please everyone and can't make decisions. When they do finally make decisions, they cancel them as soon as someone pushes back. They create loads of extra work for their teams because they can't say "no" to anyone. I can tell that I'm heading down that path. I practically shake at the thought of confronting my new boss or fighting with the other managers who are my peers. My stress level is up. My team members have started to openly show their frustration. It hasn't reached danger-zone status yet, but it's headed in that direction. This isn't good for my health or my career, but that's not the worst of it.

At home are the biggest problems. I don't want to be a Stepford Wife. When people ask me for things, in the back of my mind is always the question, "What would I want someone to say to me if I were asking for help?" The problem is that I never ask people for help, and no one in my family looks out for me the way I do for all of them. Now, as I look ahead to my daughters' teenage years, I'm beginning to wonder: Have I set them up to have no control? I never say "no" to them. That's fine when they're asking for an ice-cream cone or to stay up late to watch TV, but soon they will be asking to stay out late with boys. They'll be exposed to drinking and probably drugs.

The more I do to make them happy, the more they assume they can get away with whatever they want. I see it happening already with my eldest. If I don't start to toughen up a little, I could create real problems with my relationships with my kids. The writing is on the wall for me at home and at work. Things are only going to get worse for me if I don't change.

Karen's past provided lots of positive reinforcement for her behavior. Even her present isn't so bad. It was when Karen viewed the future that she realized how important this change was for her, her career, her health, and her relationships. As you gain perspective on your past, present, and future, you will look at a number of different areas that your behavior could affect.

Exercise 2.2 View Your Past, Present, and Future

Identify the ways your behavior affects you at home, at work, and at play. Use the following categories to spur your thinking about where the greatest impact occurs.

Health	Emotions	Finances
Relationships	Work Performance	Sleep
Career	Fun	Spirituality
Happiness	Self-Confidence	Other _____

As you answer the following questions, include both the positive and negative impacts of your behavior, and focus on the areas where you see the greatest impact:

• How has my behavior affected me in the past?

• How does my behavior affect me now?

• How will my behavior affect me in the future if I do not change?

Possibilities of Success

You have now looked at your self-addiction from the perspective of the people with whom you interact as well as your past, present, and future with this self-addiction. Now it is time to turn your attention to the possibilities of what your life will be like when you are free of these behaviors. How will your life be different? What will change?

What will be better? As you start to imagine the possibilities, be open to the most positive pictures of your future. The more positive your vision of success, the more likely that vision will keep you motivated throughout the process.

Exercise 2.3   See the Possibilities of Change

Take 15 minutes to imagine the possible outcomes that could result from successfully making your change. Picture the success in your mind and answer these questions:

• How has it changed my health, happiness and self-esteem?

• How has it changed my relationships with family, friends and coworkers?

• How has it changed my career?

Record the possibilities for success you have identified so that you can reflect on them as you continue through the process. If you were not able to see any inspiring possibilities, then come back to this exercise in a couple of hours or days to fill out your picture of success.

The clearer you are about the value of your change, the consequences of maintaining the status quo, and the broad impact of your behavior, the more dedicated you will be to the change. As you move to the next chapter, Making Meaningful Commitments, take with you any drive, any fear, any passion that you found during this chapter. Drive, fear, and passion will serve to add power to your commitments and fuel your efforts to make the change.

Make Powerful Commitments

Questions to get you started:

What are your goals?

What is going to get you through the times when you want to give up?

Fairly early in my career, I had the opportunity to go to a four-day leadership-training workshop, where I learned about exceptional leadership behaviors. I practiced these behaviors and was video-taped so that I could see just how much work I still had to do to master these skills. I left the workshop with a deep understanding of what I currently did, what the "masters" did, and what the gulf was between us. I thought I was committed to changing my behavior. I was wrong.

I told myself that I was going to become great at these skills. Why? Because I was committed to becoming a great leader. What happened? Within three months, the lessons of that workshop were a distant memory. I convinced myself that I was in fact a good, if not great, leader, and I moved on. It became easier for me to ignore

45

my commitment than to continue any effort because there was no passion in my commitment and it therefore had no power. Furthermore, it was stored away where no one could see it, making it easy to disregard and forget.

How do you make a commitment powerful?

While people have good intentions when they make commitments to change, they frequently make these commitments in a way that is fashioned to fail. Most commitments to change that people make have the power of a fly swatter over a lion. They reduce a challenging and complicated undertaking down to something little more than an errand. During your life, how many commitments have you made that sound like these?

- I'm going to go to the gym more often.
- I'm going to mow the lawn more often.
- I'm going to be more patient with my kids.
- I'm going to praise and compliment people more.
- I'm going to be more optimistic.
- I'm going to be less emotional.

You might as well say, "I'm going to run a four-minute mile." It's a nice idea. It's possible, but it's a commitment that has no teeth. Breaking a self-addiction requires a powerful commitment; building this commitment will be the goal of this chapter. When you have completed this chapter, you will have finished building your first Circle of Strength and will have created a commitment to your change that is deep, detailed, and a powerful resource to support your change effort as you go forward. Your powerful commitment will contain the following elements:

- A measurable goal
- Meaningful outcomes
- Giving up competing motives
- A time limit

- A promise to keep your attention focused on your commitment.

In the end, your powerful commitment should serve three purposes. First, it should raise your motivation to achieve your goals; second, it should create continual awareness of your objectives; and third, it should give you a chance to celebrate. When you have completed this chapter you will have clear goals with milestones you can achieve. Now is your chance to set yourself up so you can achieve a genuine sense of accomplishment and truly enjoy your success.

Measurable Goal

The first step in creating a powerful commitment is to make your goal specific and measurable. The idea here is to create your goal in such a way that you will know with certainty whether you have achieved it. A general goal says that you will do something "more" or "less." A measurable goal is precise and says that you will do something a specified number of times or in a particular way. This precision will allow you to realize if and when you are falling short of meeting or exceeding your objectives. Consider how the goals listed below could be made more specific and measurable.

Original Goal	Measurable Goal
I'm going to go to the gym more often.	I will go to the gym at least three times per week.
I'm going to mow the lawn more often.	I will mow the lawn once per week.
I'm going to be more patient with my kids.	I will have five or fewer instances of impatience with my kids per week.
I'm going to praise and compliment people more.	I will praise and/or compliment people at least twice per day.
I'm going to be more optimistic.	I will make at least one optimistic statement every day.
I'm going to be less emotional.	I will not have more than one "emotional outburst" per week.

The measurable goals leave no doubt. If you mow the lawn on Sunday, you know that you have met your goal for the week. If you wake up and tell your husband that you think today is going to be a great day, then you've met your objective of one optimistic statement for the day. On the contrary, if you get into bed at the end of the day after praising only one person that day, you know that you have fallen short.

If you go from exercising once every six months to once every three months, you will have achieved the goal of exercising "more." However, you will have hardly achieved your desired results. The measurable goal will give you a feeling of certainty in your accomplishment when you reach your goal, and will help you make adjustments when you fall short.

Sometimes, the things you do to achieve these goals will feel awkward and forced. However, you have to realize that you are building these new behaviors the same way you would build any other skill, with practice. These forced actions in the early going are only awkward because you aren't used to them yet. When you have performed the new behaviors for a while, you'll realize that you can easily meet and even exceed your goals. You may discover many more than two opportunities each day to compliment someone or to be optimistic.

It will get less awkward. It will feel more comfortable with practice, but only with practice. The measurable goal holds you accountable to practice your new behavior at the level you want to perform.

Exercise 3.1   Create a Measurable Goal

Write down your commitment to change, making it specific and measurable. Be sure to create a goal that you believe is achievable. You can always adjust your goal later in the process. Here you want to create an initial goal that will allow you to experience success. Refer to the examples in the chart on page 47 to help you create your goal.

Meaningful Outcomes

Of course, powerful commitments have to be connected to powerful convictions. It is perfectly natural for people to understand and acknowledge a "need" to change at the same time as they lack the conviction necessary to make the change. This gap between understanding and conviction creates a struggle that can last for quite a long time and is the reason many change efforts fail to reach success or, if some success was reached, fail to stick for very long.

If you feel that you are not yet convinced of the need and/or the value of your change, then go back and reread Steps 1 and 2. Search out a more meaningful change or a greater rationale for the change you have already identified. Otherwise, your powerful commitment may waver for lack of the needed conviction.

One way to connect conviction to your commitment is to anchor it in outcomes that are highly desirable for you. In the last chapter you evaluated the impact that your self-addiction has on you and the people around you. Now you can use that information by linking it to outcomes that will be meaningful to you. That is what Darrell, The Critic, did.

The Critic

I knew what I wanted to do. I wanted to be more positive and less critical of people. I wanted to let people know that I thought highly of them. I wanted to replace the criticism with praise, but what I really wanted ran a lot deeper than that.

At home I wanted my kids to feel comfortable bringing me good news or bad. I wanted my wife to feel like she didn't have to protect our kids from me. I wanted to live in a home that was open and communicative with a family that was supportive of one another. I wanted to pass on good habits to my kids so that they would build better relationships as they grew into adulthood.

At work I wanted my team members to love coming to the office. I wanted them to know about and feel confident in their strengths. I wanted to see them promoted before they chose to move out of the company. I wanted them to feel as good about working for me as I felt about having them on my team.

When Darrell made his commitments it was getting in touch with the potential benefits that made it all come alive for him. When he identified what he had to gain, he changed his whole outlook on the process. Once he pictured all of the ways his actions could change the lives of the people around him, he became far more committed to making his change.

On page 14 I pointed out that Alcoholics Anonymous recommends to members that they "change their whole lives." You may not feel that your change is quite that radical, but it is important to recognize just how significant the benefits of your change may be. Consider some of the following:

Change	Possible Benefits
Stop complaining and be more positive	Increase promotion opportunities at work Improve romantic relationships
Learn to say "no" to people's requests	Have personal time for self Relax and therefore be a better parent
Control temper and angry outbursts	Improve relationships with spouse and kids Lower blood pressure, improve health, and live a longer life

By linking your efforts to these positive benefits, you are creating a new and more powerful context for your change. "Stop complaining," may be a laudable goal, but alone it can be difficult to hold onto. However, increasing promotional opportunities and improving romantic relationships are great motivators—the sort of motivators that make it easier to hang onto the goal. When you hold a positive expectation for yourself, it makes it easier for you to achieve your results. It doesn't matter if these results seem far-fetched to you right now. The important thing is that they help you focus on a positive outcome that will motivate you to achieve your change. Reflecting on the positive builds your energy and excitement for change, and that can have powerful effects.

In the next exercise, you will identify the outcomes that are most meaningful to you. As an example, consider how Darrell did this. The impact that his critical behavior had on his relationships was broad:

- His kids were afraid to talk with him.
- His wife had to conspire against him in order to gain the trust of their children.
- His most respected workers didn't like or respect him.
- He lost his best workers to other companies.
- He made important people in his life feel bad about themselves.

Darrell's measurable commitment was:

- I will provide positive feedback at least twice per day.

However, he built on that by making these deeper commitments to meaningful outcomes:

- I will conduct myself in a way that will make my family members completely comfortable being open with me.
- I will be a manager for whom my employees love to work.
- I will retain my employees and get them promoted within the company.
- I will be the father and leader I want to be.

Exercise 3.2 Broaden Outcomes

Identify the powerful outcomes that you will create by making this change in your life.

For key people in your life (yourself, spouse/partner, kids, boss, coworkers, friends) write down commitments that you will make to improve your relationship, based on breaking your self-addiction. For reference, see Darrell's deeper commitments.

You have now begun to expand the breadth of your commitments so that they will invigorate and motivate you throughout your change process.

Remember to record your commitments in your notebook.

Competing Motives

In Step 2, Realize the Consequences, we looked at many different possible benefits you could experience if you make your change. However, if you have had difficulty changing yourself in the past, it is very likely that you currently have benefits that you gain from your present behavior. In other words, your self-addiction that hurts you in some ways rewards you in others. These rewards, which we will call competing motives, encourage you to perpetuate your current behavior. One part of making meaningful commitments is to commit to giving up these competing motives. First, let's identify what these motives are that drive your behavior.

Your self-addiction might be fueled by reinforcements that go all the way back to your childhood, or it could be driven by rewards that you continue to get today. Sometimes the underlying motives are easy to spot, sometimes not. Consider this example: I once worked with someone who wanted to stop eating sweets because after 30-plus years of maintaining a fairly consistent weight, he had put on 15 pounds. What was his motive for eating the sweets? They tasted good. He simply liked the taste. This isn't to say that motives for eating habits are always easy to figure out, but in his case, they were exactly that simple.

On the other hand, consider John, The Talker.

The Talker

There was a time when I wouldn't talk at all in group settings, but I came out of my shell years ago. Once I realized I could entertain people, it really became hard to stop. So it would have been easy for me to assume that my reason for talking was that I enjoyed entertaining. In fact, that was part of it, but there were deeper issues that I had to uncover. I had to figure out why entertaining was so important to me.

I really explored what I thought would happen if I didn't entertain. What would it be like if I sat back and didn't engage in the conversation? What if I let other people take the lead and run the discussion? The more I visualized this, the more I saw myself sinking into the background. I actually saw myself looking more and more like the geeky little kid I was when I was growing up. As I pictured this scene I saw people literally shouldering me out of the circle. I became an undesirable.

As soon as I described the scenario I knew it wasn't fair. My friends and colleagues wouldn't push me away like that if I talked less, and I certainly wouldn't become the geeky kid I once was. Seeing that picture gave me a new way to view the change. Now, when I try not to talk as much, I find it interesting to see how people are responding to me. Before I was always looking for the laugh. Now I look for signs of respect.

John realized that his motives ran deeper than simply enjoying talking or wanting to hear himself talk. He saw that there were multiple levels and types of needs that encouraged his speaking. Motives can be straightforward, or they can have many layers. They can come from rewards of the present situation, or they can be rooted in experiences from long ago. They may be purely about you, or they may be about relationships you have had throughout your lifetime. Below are some self-addictions and motives that can drive them.

Self-Addiction	Motive
Defensiveness	You fear that you or your actions will be viewed as ignorant or stupid. Your defensiveness helps you justify your actions and protects you from being wrong.
Self-Victimization	You are afraid that you are incompetent and that you have made serious errors. By seeing yourself as the victim of challenging circumstances or other people's actions, you don't have to confront your own inabilities.
Controlling Others	You are afraid that others will hurt themselves or you. Controlling them takes away their ability to do any harm.
Negative Attitude	When things don't go the way you want them to go, you become afraid that they will get worse. You take a negative attitude to reduce your expectations and to protect yourself from further disappointment. You may also use your negative attitude to build camaraderie with other angry or embittered people.

These are just a few examples of how self-addictions can link to underlying motives, and the ones shown aren't the only motives that can apply to these self-addictions. In order to identify your own motives, you will need to ask yourself some tough questions and be prepared to provide the honest answers. There are many layers to your motives. Each one that you uncover will give you a clearer path to how to battle your self-addiction.

Once you identify your competing motives, you will need to make meaningful commitments to give up these motives. Consider the following examples:

Example 1

Maria wants to lose weight. She commits to a diet and exercise routine. However, she has competing desires to sleep and to maintain a casual lifestyle that is free of rigid routines. She commits to waking up earlier in order to make time for her exercise. Furthermore, she commits to accepting some rigidity in her life so that she can create consistency with her exercise and with her food shopping.

Example 2

Randall doesn't show his emotions. The women he dates describe him as cold and as a result, do not stay with him for long. Randall prides himself on his logic and objectivity. However, his self-image reinforces his cold demeanor. To change his behavior Randall commits to be open about his feelings in his next relationship. Unfortunately, he has competing desires to be in control and invulnerable. He is afraid that he will look weak or stupid if he talks about his emotions. Randall has to accept that it will be okay if he talks about an emotion that his girlfriend finds strange. So Randall commits to the risk that his girlfriend will think poorly of him if he is awkward in expressing his emotions.

Example 3

Pat complains about everything. She commits to stop complaining, but she has a competing desire to get attention. Every time she complains at home and at work, people listen to her. She is the proverbial squeaky wheel that gets the oil. Complaining is her way to be significant. In order to release herself from her competing desires, she commits to three things. First, she commits to ask more questions of people. Second, she commits to do things to make others feel good. She believes that both of these actions will get her noticed in a positive way. Third, she commits to give up her need for attention if it requires her to be negative.

Competing motives will always work to pull you back into your old behaviors. They counteract any work that you do to make yourself a better person. By identifying them and pledging to overcome them, you better position yourself to make your change and stick with it over time.

The objective for the next exercise is to identify your competing motives and make commitments to counteract them. Competing motives are not always easy to identify and sometimes have many layers of depth. In the exercise, you should challenge yourself to dig deeper into each answer. Every time you answer a question, stop, think about it, and answer it again. Identifying your competing motives will help you break down a major source of resistance to your success.

Exercise 3.3   Identify Competing Motives
Answer the following questions to identify your competing motives: • Why do I do what I do?   • What do I gain from my behavior?   • What am I afraid would happen if I didn't continue my behavior?   • What would happen if I did the opposite of this behavior?   Once you feel that you have a clear understanding of your competing motives, write down in your notebook commitments to break them. Use the examples above of Maria, Randall, and Pat as models to follow. Your commitments should include statements to give up behaviors, beliefs, and/or any self-image you have that will hold you back from your goals.

If you have difficulty with this exercise, try talking through it with a trusted friend, or come back to it later. Uncovering these insights frequently takes time combined with other people's perspectives.

At this point, it is important to recognize how far you have come. The commitments you have made so far in this chapter may seem overwhelming. They may entail a lot of work, and that can be scary. Now is the moment to take heart and celebrate what you have already done. By working through these exercises, you are taking this process seriously and moving effectively down the path to your change.

Time Limit

Committing to time means defining a period during which you will work on your change. Most people who try to change commit to their new actions "from now on." Their commitment is forever. Unfortunately, "forever" commitments don't work. Don't get me wrong; I want you to make your change for good. I want it to be permanent, but committing to do something from now on doesn't make it happen. In fact, if your commitment is forever then you can't actually achieve your goal until you die. That's a pretty depressing milestone.

Therefore, I will recommend that you commit to a specific time for your change. On New Year's Eve, don't commit to changing forever. Commit to changing for January. Committing to a finite period makes your efforts more achievable and easier to hold onto. When you find it difficult to continue your efforts, you don't have to face the prospect of eternity. Just look at the calendar. It's January 23? That's fantastic! You only need to continue for eight more days.

The time of your commitment is a starting point. When you reach the end of your commitment you will be able to determine whether to continue. You will have the opportunity to make that decision intentionally instead of simply drifting back to your old habits because "forever" is too much to handle.

The next exercise is short, but meaningful. Your commitment here will give you a goal toward which you can direct your energy. Make your time goal challenging but achievable. You want to make a commitment that will allow you to experience success. You may also struggle during the time period that you set. That's okay. The time period you establish shouldn't feel easy, but neither should it feel overwhelming. It should be a challenging stretch for you to begin and continue your new behaviors for the entire time.

Exercise 3.4 Commit to Time

Commit to a specific amount of time within which you will work on changing your behavior. In general, I recommend one month, but you may want a shorter time period if you are battling a particularly challenging self-addiction. Identify a specific end date for your commitment.

Once you commit to a date, block out a time on your calendar on that date to determine your readiness to recommit. When we discuss maintenance of changes in Step 9, we will discuss what to do on that date. For now, just mark the date down and reserve the time. The mark on your calendar will serve as an extra motivator and reminder to stick with your efforts.

Commitment to Attention

Your final commitment is to attention. By that I mean that you need to make a commitment to paying attention to your change and remaining aware of the effort you are undertaking. I was recently describing self-addiction to a group of people and discussing the relative ineffectiveness of most commitments and most efforts to change. It was mid-January and we were laughing at the futility of New Year's resolutions. To drive the point home, everyone revealed their resolutions and what they had done. In fact, most had done nothing, hadn't even thought about the resolutions since midnight on New Year's Eve. A few of the people couldn't even remember what their resolutions had been.

The systems they used to make and keep their commitments didn't work. Part of the reason they were unable to keep their commitments was that they made them too easy to forget. The commitments were out of sight and out of mind in less time than it took the ball to drop in Times Square. There are many ways to increase the attention you pay to your commitments. Consider how your attention to your commitments would increase if you did each of the following:

- Think of a change you'd like to make.
- Verbally commit to yourself that you will make the change.
- Write down your commitment
- Place your written commitment where you will see it regularly and/or create a routine to reread your commitment daily.
- Share your commitment with others and ask them to ask you about your progress.

Most New Year's resolutions stop at the first or second bullet on this list. There is nothing tangible, no physical reminder of the pledge; therefore when we forget, there is nothing to bring us back and reinforce the commitments we made. It's up to our memories. Maybe we'll remember. Maybe we won't. Maybe we'll remember, commit again, and forget again. The more we depend on *maybes* to make significant changes in our lives, the more we are setting ourselves up to fail, which is exactly what Susan, The Worker, had done in the past.

The Worker

After I cross-examined my husband and realized how big an impact my work was having on my whole family, I really wanted to make this change different. So I looked back at the New Year's resolutions I had made in the past, the ones where I said, "I'll spend more time with my family." When I thought about how I made these resolutions and what I did with them, I realized that I never took them seriously.

When something important comes up at work, I have a whole process for ensuring that I am successful. If I recognize that a client is particularly needy, I will schedule extra time with her to calm her fears.

I will continue this for as long as needed, and that's the real catch. I evaluate their needs in what I call my "Active Client Review Meetings." Once a week I sit down to determine needed actions for any clients with whom I am currently working. I keep a list of those clients by my desk so that I continually think about what they need and what I have to deliver. My weekly meeting and my list keep all of my clients and especially the neediest of them at the top of my mind.

My family was another story. Every New Year's I would make a resolution to spend more time with them. I'd book a vacation and make a couple of restaurant reservations. We'd have our "family time." I'd assuage my guilt, and then I would forget, at least until the following New Year's Eve.

It's not that the resolution wasn't important. I just got busy at work, where I always was. Knowing how I care for my clients, I know that I could have taken my resolutions more seriously. If I had paid attention to my family's needs the way I did my clients', things would have been different. Instead, I was all too happy to forget my resolutions and brush them under the rug. I knew that once I got them out of my mind, I wouldn't have to worry about them again until next year.

Susan's story points out the ease with which you can set yourself up to forget and let your commitments slip away. She also points out that sometimes people want to forget. You are at a critical time in your change process. To succeed in your change, you must not only want the change, but you must be committed to overcoming the challenge that you will face in making the change. In the past, Susan didn't want to face these things. She wanted to forget.

In the following exercise, the last in the Circle of Awareness section of the book, you will make sure that you don't forget your commitments to change. You will compile your final meaningful commitment and keep it in front of you for the next month. Compiling your commitment simply means writing down in one concise package the commitments that have come out of this chapter. These commitments will include:

- Your goal

- How it will change your relationships

- What you will give up

- The timeline for your commitment

- When you will read the commitment.

Here is an example of a meaningful commitment from Darrell, The Critic:

> I will provide positive feedback at least twice per day . . . so that my family members will be completely comfortable being open with me and my employees will love to work for me . . . I will allow myself to not know all of the answers and to not control all of the outcomes . . . for the next month . . . I will read this statement every morning.

Your meaningful commitment will maintain your awareness of what is most important and keep you on track to make your change.

Exercise 3.5   Make Your Powerful Commitment
Compile your own meaningful commitment. Place a written statement of your commitment where it will be visible to you. Here are some suggested locations:

PDA	Car radio	Refrigerator
Personal Calendar	Bathroom mirror	Front door
Outlook Calendar	Bookmark	Television
Nightstand	Computer/desk	Stereo

You may also want to share your commitments with other people, which can be a great help in strengthening your resolve. If you are unsure about whether (or how) to talk to people about your change efforts, keep in mind that this topic will be discussed thoroughly in the next section of the book, Building Support.

The Circle of Awareness

You have now completed the Circle of Awareness. You have built a base of information and awareness about what your addiction is, how it affects your life, and what commitments you are ready to make in order to break your self-addiction. The circle is an important concept to keep in mind as you move to the next section. When you move in a circle, you keep on coming back to your starting point. So it should be with your Circle of Awareness.

Awareness can fade with time if it is not refreshed. Even important self-realizations and commitments can be forgotten if they are not attended to. This tendency to forget about new ideas makes your final commitment the most important of all. Breaking a self-addiction takes time. During that time, to prevent yourself from lapsing back into old behaviors and forgetting your change effort, keep a consistent routine for reviewing your commitments. Doing so will keep you on the right track for making your change.

In order to break your self-addiction, you will need more than awareness. You will also need the various people in your life to help you in your efforts. That is the topic we turn to next as we examine the Circle of Support.

Part II

Building Support

In this section you will build a Circle of Support so that others can help you build the strength to change. Whether it is from pride or out of fear of embarrassment or commitment, many people are reluctant to ask others for help when making personal changes. Yet, almost everyone is surrounded by people who care about them and would be happy to help them change. Over the next few chapters you will explore who might be appropriate candidates to support you and how to engage them in your change efforts. Specifically, you will look at three different processes by which you can build your Circle of Support.

Step 4: Find Help
Identify supporters among your family, friends,
and coworkers and determine possible roles for them
to play in support of your change.

Step 5: Invite Support
Develop strategies to approach your supporters,
request their help, and create a positive, effective relationship.

Step 6: Maintain Support
Explore how to evaluate your support relationships,
make adjustments, and sustain effective relationships over time.

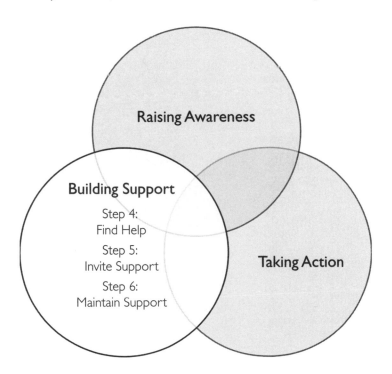

Raising Awareness

Building Support

Step 4:
Find Help

Step 5:
Invite Support

Step 6:
Maintain Support

Taking Action

Circles of Strength

Find Help

Questions to get you started:

Who helps you?

What are all the different ways that people support you?

How can your friends, family, and coworkers help you make a change?

I used to have a problem. I didn't know when to keep my mouth shut. I challenged authority more than was healthy for me or my career. Fortunately, someone helped me overcome my behavioral addiction. He was a colleague of mine and also a good friend. At first, he just pointed things out to me after they'd happened. We'd have lunch after a team meeting and he'd say to me, "Do you know that you shouldn't have said that the new policy is stupid?" I'd tell him that I realized it after the fact, and that would be that. We'd have a meeting. I'd say something challenging to my manager or about senior management. My friend would admonish me for it afterward, and I'd keep on doing what I was doing. I was finding it beyond my power to stop the behavior on my own.

Then he did something different. He sat next to me in a meeting, and every time he saw me getting frustrated, he would step on my foot. He knew the signs that meant I was about to say something detrimental to my career. It worked. It stopped me and forced me to think about what I wanted to say. I still challenged things when I felt strongly enough about them, but my challenges were more thoughtful and less antagonistic. We should all be so lucky to have friends who voluntarily step up to support our needs. The simple truth is that significant change requires help.

What do you need to consider in order to find help?

In this section we will explore various ways to build a network of support to help you break your self-addiction. Step 4 will address:

- The value of support
- How trust plays into support
- Who your possible supporters could be
- What roles they can play
- How some people play contrary roles and undermine your efforts to change.

The Value of Support

You will benefit from support in many ways. Supporters can offer you feedback, both critical and positive, on how you are doing relative to your goals. They can also provide you with unique perspectives. They can turn you around when you get down on yourself and point out your successes. Your supporters can ground you and help you see what is really happening in your change efforts.

A partner in your change efforts can also challenge and push you to greater performance and help you come up with new ideas for how to perform better in the future. Alcoholics Anonymous uses this support to guide its members. When a new person joins, he is encouraged to find a sponsor. The sponsor is someone who helps the new member navigate the steps of the program and manage the situations that could lead to relapse. Without the sponsor, the program wouldn't be nearly as effective.

Also, when you are alone and you fail to achieve your goals, there is no one with whom you can share your disappointment. When you involve other people, you create an important motivation that could help you make your change. People who are counting on you or rooting for you help you remain accountable and motivated so you work harder to avoid disappointing them. I've known many people who wouldn't think twice about disappointing themselves, but disappointing other people would cause them tremendous angst. Building a support network can help fuel this type of motivation.

There is also a risk when you lack supporters that your success goes underappreciated. You can't expect that the first time you change your behavior, everyone around you will notice your change, stop what they are doing, and give you a standing ovation. In all likelihood, you will be the only one who notices. Karen, The Pushover, tells her story of this experience.

The Pushover

When I committed to giving up my pushover behavior, I thought that people would really take notice. I remember a meeting I had with my department. We would have these big meetings with my boss and all of my peers and all of the people who reported to us. My boss always had new work to assign in these meetings, and he always asked for volunteers. I was always the first to raise my hand, and my team had started to dread these meetings because of that. During this meeting I counted the places where I would have jumped to volunteer in the past. There were 10 different times that I would have taken on a thankless task or project.

After the meeting, I looked for any sign of recognition from my team, any hint that they realized that this discussion was different. In the end, they didn't seem to notice anything. I wanted to stand up and shout at them, "Don't you realize how different things are? Don't you understand how hard I'm trying for you?" But they didn't. It was really disheartening at first. Then I tried to see it from their perspective.

They've got this boss who's always been a pain in the neck. I offer up their time even when they're stretched thin. I ask them for "favors" because I somehow think that will make it okay that I've once again agreed to something that will make their work miserable. I put off difficult decisions because I don't want to upset anyone. Of course, that just makes people more upset.

All of a sudden a conversation went by where I didn't volunteer their time for everything. To them, this was an aberration. Maybe they thought I didn't get enough sleep last night and wasn't really listening. Maybe they thought that I was having family problems and was distracted during the discussion. Maybe they didn't think anything at all, because they didn't even notice. I expected them to do cartwheels because they'd had one good meeting with me. Meanwhile, for them, this was only one good meeting out of the last 100.

Karen thought that any change in her behavior that she noticed would also be noticed by those around her. She assumed that the same people who were frustrated with her would turn around and recognize and appreciate her for taking her first steps to make their situation better. The truth is that when you try to change, you will be much more aware of any minor adjustments in your action than those around you. The people around you are used to seeing you in the way they always have seen you. It is only once you make big changes and sustain them over time that others will see your progress and give you credit.

One opportunity that you have is to bring people into your process. Let them know what you are doing. Then they will be more on the lookout and more likely to see the changes you make. It is important to celebrate your successes along the way. You will be much better able to enjoy the moment if you have partners with whom you can share your triumphs.

The Trust Factor

We will look in more detail at the different types of partners, how to identify people to help you, and how to ask those individuals for support. However, before we get to that, it is important to understand how trust issues play into these relationships. By telling people about your commitments to change, you become vulnerable. You are vulnerable because you have shared that you have a flaw and have opened yourself up to criticism if you fail to change. At this point, you may even be wondering, "Why should I trust other people with my change?"

The truth is that if you don't trust someone to act honorably and help you change, then you probably shouldn't invite that person to be a partner. However, if you don't trust anyone to act honorably and help you change, then you should probably reexamine yourself and your ability to trust. That's what John, The Talker, went through.

The Talker

I was embarrassed. It's not like other people didn't know that I talked a lot, but I was embarrassed to come out and say that I knew, too. I felt if I said it, it would be like saying that I knew I was a jerk or an annoyance or a blowhard. It would be like saying to everyone, "I know that you don't really like spending time with me." That just hurt. I really wanted to stay in my fake world where everyone pretended to ignore everyone else's inadequacies and annoying quirks.

Besides, even if I could get past the embarrassment, this was a big career issue for me. I didn't want to just come out and tell my colleagues that I had a "problem behavior." That kind of information can come back to haunt you in a political organization like mine. I worked with a couple of people who were real snakes. They'd stab you in the back in a heartbeat.

There was one guy in particular who I really didn't trust. I imagined what he would do if I talked to him about this. I envisioned elaborate scenarios in which he would use the information to prevent me from getting promoted, to get my name taken off important committees, to stop me from getting other opportunities in the company. The more I thought about this guy, the more nervous I got.

Then it finally hit me and I knew what I was doing. I was using the worst case scenario to generalize about everyone I knew. My assessment of this guy may or may not have been accurate, but it certainly was not an accurate depiction of how my other colleagues would act. I knew a lot of people who cared about me and wanted to see me succeed. They were the partners I needed to seek. I allowed myself to get so wrapped up in my fears of what the snake would do that I failed to see the good things that others would be able to do.

John came to an important realization that there were people he could trust and people he couldn't trust. His situation is similar to most. You probably know at least one or two people who are untrustworthy, can't keep a secret, don't care about you, and wouldn't think twice about hurting you if it served their purposes. However, you probably know many more people who do care about you and who want to see you succeed.

Your challenge is to separate those who are trustworthy from those who are not. Once you do, you will find that trusting people and inviting them into your process creates benefits that are well worth the risks. Breaking your self-addiction is worth the vulnerability of sharing your development process. Developing a stronger relationship with the person because of this connection outweighs the discomfort and insecurity that it creates for you. You will also see that these are benefits that may come to your supporters as well.

I coached a woman who was trying to start a new exercise routine. When we began our work, she didn't believe that anyone would simply want to help her. She thought that if she asked someone to help her, it would be a burden to them and they would resent her for asking. In fact, she thought these things because she was wrapped up in what this process meant to her. She never really considered what it could mean to someone else.

We weren't talking about major commitments. All we were

discussing was asking one of her friends, a caring person who was something of an exercise buff, to ask her about her progress each week. They spoke on the phone regularly anyway. We were just considering dedicating a couple of minutes of those conversations to her workout progress, but she was dead set against it. Then I turned the tables.

I asked her what she would do if her friend asked her for help. What would she do if her friend asked her to do something that would take no more than five minutes each week, but would help him immensely? It was a no-brainer. Of course she would help. When I asked why, she had many reasons:

- She cared about her friend.

- It would make her feel good to be helpful.

- It might motivate her or give her insights for her own change.

- It was a minimal commitment for a powerful reward.

There are probably people in your life who aren't trustworthy, but most people are. Not only are most people willing and able to help, but most will also receive benefits just from supporting your efforts. Alcoholics Anonymous figured this out with their sponsorship process. Far from being a burden, becoming a sponsor for someone else is actually a privilege that helps members complete the final steps of the process. By helping others, they actually help themselves.

Potential Supporters

Your goal in identifying partners is to identify as many people as you can who may be able to support your change. This is a brainstorming activity. Your objective is not to evaluate the names as they come to you. Rather, you want to identify as many names as you can. The longer your list, the more likely you will be to find partners who fit your needs. Include in your list your family members, friends, and colleagues who may be able to help you.

Write down all the people you can think of who might be able to help you
make your change. Take at least five minutes to identify these people.

Once you have completed your list, the next step will be to determine who on that list to ask for support, and what kind of partnership to form with each person. Remember that different people are
right for different roles. It isn't about the person so much as it is
about your relationship to the person. I had an experience once in
which I saw this contrast in a very personal way.

I met my wife in graduate school where she was studying for
her PhD in psychology. A few years later I became good friends with
another PhD candidate in a different program. My friend asked me
if I could coach her to help her work toward the completion of her
degree. I was thrilled to support this process and agreed readily. At
the same time that I was coaching my friend, I saw my wife struggling with many of the same issues. Attaining a PhD is an extremely
difficult task, and it pained me to watch her go through such a tough
time. However, I was limited in how I could help her.

For my friend I could play many roles. I could push and challenge her and question her actions and decisions. I could give her
advice and we could work together to develop action plans and strategies. For my wife I had to play a very different role. I couldn't push or
challenge her. She pushed herself so hard and put so much pressure
on herself that she needed something else from me. She needed me
to play more of a compassionate role. I had to be supportive of her at
all times, but especially when she felt overwhelmed. The one thing I
absolutely couldn't do was pressure her the way I did my friend.

This is not a flaw in my relationship with my wife. It is simply
an indication of how I could best help her achieve her goals. Sometimes people are too close to or too far from the issues for you to feel
comfortable with them in certain roles. You may have a great role
for your friend to play that you couldn't possibly ask your mom to
play. Your brother may be able to do something for you that your

coworker cannot. You need to recognize what you most need from each individual to get the best support out of the relationship.

Supporting Roles

We will look at three different levels of support. Each has a certain depth to the relationship, and the deeper that relationship is, the more power it has to affect your change. These three types of partners are illustrated in the graph below.

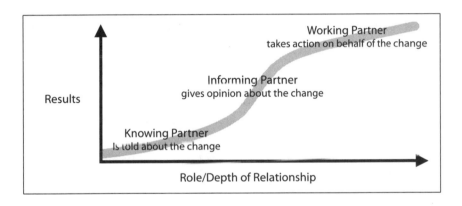

The Knowing Partner

A knowing partner is simply anyone who knows what change you are trying to make. You tell them about your change. They know what you are trying to do, but they don't have any defined role in the process. If they do something, it is by their own design. A knowing partner can be anyone—friends, family, coworkers, your cab driver, or the checkout person at the supermarket. They merely need to hear your statement to play their role. Of course, the closer to you they are, the more their knowing is likely to influence your behavior. Having knowing partners can certainly help, but they are the weakest social support that you can create.

The Informing Partner

Informing partners give you their opinions about your change. These supporters are ones whom you tell about your efforts and ask to give you feedback on your performance. For these to be truly effective, you should make plans to speak with them regularly about your progress. Frequently, people create informing partners by saying something like, "I'm trying to be less defensive. I'd like you to let me know how I'm doing." Then they walk away and never discuss the matter again. It's much more effective when the individual says, "I'm trying to be less defensive. I'd like to meet with you once a week to hear your observations on how I am doing." An informing partner should be someone who can observe you in action. It does little good for you to ask for feedback on your behavior from someone who rarely or never sees you exhibit the behavior in question.

If you are willing to consistently ask for feedback, you will do a much better job of accomplishing your goals. Consistent feedback is not the same as extensive feedback. In fact, you can ask for this information in very brief conversations of only a few minutes duration. The key is to conduct these conversations consistently.

The Working Partner

Working partners are people who actually take action on your behalf to help you make the change. They may stop you when they see you engaging in the addictive behavior, as the friend I described at the beginning of this chapter did for me. Working partners can also be those who help you think through your actions and develop strategies for building new behaviors. If you have talked through any of the exercises in this book with someone else, that person was acting as a working partner. A working partner can also be someone who is going through the same change effort as you. For example, someone who goes with you to the gym to exercise can be a working partner.

A working partner can do a lot of things to help you succeed, but there is one thing that makes this partnership particularly valuable. The working partner will share the burden of the change with you. Making meaningful and lasting change is a challenging and prolonged process and you are bound to face setbacks along the way. Working partners help you to keep going, to get past the difficult times, and to achieve your goals.

Here are four different types of working partners:

Thinker—someone who will help you think through plans and strategies for your change.

Challenger—someone who will push you to higher levels of achievement.

Supporter—someone who will provide you with positive feedback and encouragement.

Actor—someone who is with you and will act to help you alter your self-addictive behavior the moment you engage in it.

Each of the above roles can be distinct from one another, or someone could play multiple roles. Following are some of the roles I asked people to play in helping me to write this book.

Person	Role
Wife	Supporter and Actor—encourage me throughout the process; take care of the kids at night and on weekends when I most need writing time.
Brother	Challenger and Informing Partner—push me to create and stick to a writing schedule; review and edit each chapter.
Editor	Thinker and Informing Partner—help me to think through content; review and edit each chapter.
Writing Coach	Challenger and Thinker—push me to stretch my goals for the writing and for what the book could be; help me to think through content.

These weren't all of the partners involved in the process, but they are good examples of people who played tremendous roles in helping me develop the writing behaviors and discipline that made this book possible. In the next exercise you will review your list of names of possible supporters and determine the roles each person can play.

Exercise 4.2   Create Roles

Go through your list of possible partners and create roles that each one could play. Try to identify at least two people as informing partners and at least two as working partners. You do not have to assign a role to everyone on your list of possible partners. In fact, if there are people on your list whom you do not trust, now is the time to remove them from the process.

   Don't ask them for this support yet. The next chapter will provide strategies for creating an effective support relationship.

Addiction Enablers

You have now started to build your own Circle of Support. The next chapter will detail how to approach your partners and develop effective relationships to support your change. However, there is a flip side to the support coin. As you have examined the people in your life who may be able to help you make your change, you may also have come across people who will make it difficult for you to change. There will inevitably be people who make it easy for you, even encourage you, to engage in your self-addictions. These people are addiction enablers, and they come in many forms.

- **The Coconspirator** does it with you. These are the people who take a break with you to go smoke a cigarette. These could be people who are always willing to join in when you want to be angry, bitter, and negative. Coconspirators share your self-addiction and make it easier for you to maintain the behavior.

- **The Pessimist** believes that you can't teach an old dog new tricks. They just don't think people change. Pessimists make it easy for you to choose not to do anything about your self-addiction because they convince you that it would all be a wasted effort anyway.

- **The Admirer** tells you that whatever you're doing isn't so bad. They may say, "Don't get so down on yourself. You're a great person." Admirers are incapable of saying anything critical. They love to compliment you and make you feel great about yourself, even if that stops you from making improvements in your life.

- **The Avoider** turns the other cheek and pretends that the behavior doesn't exist. They may get angry or frustrated with you on the inside, but they won't let you know.

Each of these addiction enablers makes it difficult for you to break your self-addictions, but that doesn't make them bad people. In fact, in their own ways they may be trying to help. It's just that they don't realize how their actions actually hurt you. They simply don't know that they have the opposite effect from what you desire. The good news is, they are likely more than happy to do something differently so they can help you. You just need to tell them about it. When I was a smoker I had lots of coconspirators who would actively encourage me to join them for a cigarette or to buy in bulk to reduce the cost. When I told them that I was quitting, they turned their behavior around and refused to let me have any of their cigarettes if I asked. They went from coconspirators to working partners.

In some cases, you will be able to easily change the behaviors of your addiction enablers. In others, their behaviors will be too entrenched to change, and your challenge will be to negate their messages. There are three ways in which you can limit or eliminate the impact of your addiction enablers. First, you can avoid them. The simplest solution (assuming the addiction enabler isn't someone important to you) is simply to reduce your exposure to them.

Second, you can try to change them. You can ask them to change their behaviors and help you make your change. This can be a good strategy, but you will need to watch to make sure they are playing the role you want them to play and not sliding back into enabling your addictions.

Third, you can change the way you respond to their behavior. If you know what kind of addiction enabler they are, you can adjust your response based on that knowledge. With the Pessimist, the Admirer, and the Avoider, you will need to remind yourself that they don't own the truth. When you speak with them, it is important to avoid getting sucked into their version of reality. You need to remember that change is more possible than what the Pessimist says. Your behavior is more important than what the Admirer tells you. The Avoider is more affected by your behavior than she lets on. If you prepare yourself with this knowledge, then you can construct your own version of the truth to fuel your efforts.

The Coconspirators are different in that they push you into your addictive behaviors in the moment. They offer you a donut when you're on a diet. They invite you to join them in their misery when you are trying to be more optimistic and positive. With the Coconspirators you can begin with this strategy: just say "no." In Steps 7 and 8 we will discuss at greater length different strategies for preparing yourself to avoid your addictive behaviors and achieve new, more positive behaviors. For now, here is an example of how someone trying to break the addiction to a short temper dealt with her addiction enablers.

Name	Enabler Type	Basic Strategy	Additional Ideas
James (husband)	Coconspirator	Change him	Invite him to be a working partner so that we can both work on this together to improve our marriage and the example we set for our kids.
Sue (friend)	Pessimist	Change my response	Always ask Sue, "What's the best that could happen?" to force us both to remember the possibilities and what is at stake.
Patrick (brother)	Admirer	Avoid the topic	Don't avoid him, but avoid the topic of my temper with him. Don't let him talk me into feeling okay about it.
Julie (coworker)	Avoider	Change my response	Ask Julie to be an informing partner. This way I will have to ask her regularly about how I am treating her and challenge my own assumption that everything is okay.

The next exercise will help you to identify the addiction enablers in your life. Then you will think through strategies for addressing each of them.

Exercise 4.3   Disable Your Addiction Enablers

Construct a chart like the one on page 78. Identify people who play each enabler role in your life (Coconspirator, Pessimist, Admirer, Avoider). Keep in mind that some of the roles may be played by multiple people, some people may play multiple roles, and some roles may not be played by anyone. Then come up with at least one strategy for each of the addiction enablers you have identified.

Surrounding With Support

You should now have a clear picture of the people who surround you. You should know which of them can open up new possibilities for helping you to change. You should also see who around you might cause you to slip back into bad behaviors. Understanding the players is the first step. The next step will be approaching each of these individuals, asking for their support, and coaching them in how they can best help you make your change. That is the topic of Step 5, Invite Support.

Invite Support

Questions to get you started:

How do you ask people for help?

How do you create an effective support relationship?

For support to be effective, it must be delivered in a way that actually helps you. In order for that to happen, you and your supporter should be equal partners, both having a voice in how you can change and how to make the support relationship work. Early in my career I was on a team in which we failed to create this equality and subsequently failed each other as supporters.

All of the members of my team strived to provide exceptional support to one another. We all prided ourselves on our ability to give one another feedback. We talked about continuously improving our skills and supporting one another's development, and it turned out it wasn't just talk. We did it. We gave each other feedback all the time, after meetings and presentations, on our writing and speaking, one-on-one, and in group settings. There was no topic, no time, and no place that was off limits, and it was all in the name of helping our team succeed.

I was on a business trip to Miami with three of my team members, two of whom were new to the team, when one of the flaws in our support system became glaringly obvious. We had just finished a long day of client meetings and were sitting down to dinner at an outdoor café. It was warm. There were palm trees swaying in the breeze. Our cocktails had just been served. I was exhausted. And then we did what we always did after a day of meetings: we reviewed the meetings and each of our actions, looking for what was done well and what could be improved. Unfortunately, on that day, at that moment, in that atmosphere, when the discussion came around to critiquing my actions, I wasn't in the mood.

I just wanted to sip my drink, listen to the palm trees, and have a nice, relaxing dinner. But that's not how our system was designed. Our feedback system was designed so that when someone wanted to give you feedback, your job was to listen. I wasn't in the mood. I fought the feedback. I rejected anything that was critical. I tuned it out if I didn't need to respond. I set a lousy example for the new team members, and I made all of them nervous about giving me feedback in the future.

How do you create effective support relationships?

The circumstances have to be right for support and feedback to have their intended results. We all are far more welcoming of some sorts of advice over others. We welcome some questions, but not all. There are times when we are receptive, and times when we are not. Finally, there are people whose feedback we welcome and others whose feedback is difficult for us to accept.

Step 5, Inviting Support, will show you how to:

1. Position the request so that your supporters feel eager to help.

2. Define the support so that it works for you and your supporter.

The problem with my team's system was that feedback was the goal. We said that we were striving for individual and team development, but in the end we placed delivering the feedback ahead of helping the person. We didn't care how ready or able the other person was to hear our message. What was important was the right we each had to deliver the message.

Your challenge in inviting supporters to help you with your change is to invite them in a way that makes your relationship productive for your goals. This is a tricky process. You have to invite people in a way that gives you enough control over the situation that you will want to receive their support, and gives them enough flexibility that they will want to provide the support. It isn't enough simply to ask someone to help. You have to make the request in a way that it truly supports your needs. Here is what Darrell discovered.

The Critic

I was really committed to changing my ways and wanted to start right away. I told everyone I could about what I was trying to do and asked them to let me know if I came across as critical. At first this was helpful. I got called on a couple of comments where I was heavy-handed with people. That was great, but it didn't take long for this to go overboard. Pretty soon all of these people who were supposed to be helping me were stifling every comment I made.

All of a sudden I couldn't make even the slightest suggestion without being told that I was being critical. The truth was that I needed to be critical. I was a manager and a father. There were times when my responsibilities required that I criticize things, but there was no way to differentiate between good criticism and bad criticism. So then I started fighting back against the very people whom I had asked for help. Then I was told that I was being even more critical because of the way I defended myself.

I created a terrible cycle in which two things became very clear to me. The first was that people could definitely help me. The people I asked for help were all too happy to let me know when they thought

> I had messed up. The second was that I needed a better system for
> how to use this help. I needed a much better plan for how and when
> I would seek input from the people around me.

Darrell's system and my old team's system were both flawed. They
both made the receiver of the feedback powerless. These were not
partnerships. Rather, they were one-way streets designed to satisfy
the person delivering the feedback, not to provide maximum support to the person receiving the feedback. Darrell needed something
in his system that would allow him to discuss his actions without
being labeled as defensive. In my old team we needed a hold but-
ton. Our members needed the right, on occasion, to hold off on the
feedback until the next day.

Position Your Request

Your supporters need to know that you really want their help, that
their help is important because you respect them, and that you will
be open to their input, or it will be all too easy for them to disregard your request for help. In order for you to convince someone to
help you, you need to overcome some possible sources of resistance.
Consider the following concerns about trusting your motives and
commitment:

- No way am I going to tell him what he's really doing. For
  what? So he can bite my head off and hold it against me
  that I criticized him?

- He doesn't really want help. He just wants to feel better
  about himself. He's just saying he wants to know to convince himself that he's not as bad as he is.

- He doesn't want to change. He's just asking for my input
  because it will make him look like he's trying to improve.

Or how about the concern your supporter may have about his
ability to deliver a tough message:

- I hate doing this. It's just going to make him feel bad.

I can't stand to see someone beat themselves up over something like this.

When you ask for support, you are asking people to step out of their own comfort zones. To do this successfully you have to ask in such a way that they will be truly committed to the actions you request of them. Even those who agree to your request may very well be reluctant to carry out their commitments. You can improve your chances of success by positioning the request in a way that appeals to their pride and displays the strength of your commitment to the change.

Before you ask someone for support, it is important to prepare yourself for the conversation. You want to make your request in the best way possible to set yourself up for success. To do so you will prepare a script that will meet your supporters' three basic needs. Your supporters need to know that:

- You really do want their help.
- You want their help because you truly value their opinions.
- You will be open to their input when it is offered.

Here is a sample script for how this request might be expressed:

Hi Gerald,

I wanted to ask you for some help on a personal project I'm working on right now. I've come to realize that I avoid even the slightest disagreements and confrontations. I don't think this is good for me or the people around me, and I'd like to change my behavior. I'd like to do a better job of recognizing when I am uncomfortable discussing something and addressing the issue.

I was hoping you could help me in this effort. I'm asking you because I really value your opinion and have always appreciated the feedback you've given me in the past. I don't think that I can change this on my own. I'm asking you for help, because I think it will give me a much better chance of achieving my goals. I do realize that it might be awkward for you to help me in this effort, but you should know that I am committed to this and fully open to your suggestions and help.

What do you think? Would you be willing to help me do this?

Exercise 5.1   Script Your Request

Write down your own script for requesting support. Be sure that your script conveys the three key points: (1) you sincerely want their help, (2) you value their opinion, and (3) you will be open to their input.

The script from this exercise will be the first half of a discussion guide that you will develop in this chapter. The second half of the guide will be developed in the next exercise.

Define the Support

Once someone has expressed willingness to help you, it is important to discuss what kind of help you are asking of them. In the last chapter you identified different roles that you would like to ask people to play. Now is the time to discuss those roles with your supporters to determine how they will best be able to support your efforts. Your goal here is not to assign them their role. Rather, it is to offer one possible option and explore the best solutions. You may go in hoping for one type of support and identify a completely different way that the individual can help you. By making this a conversation instead of an assignment, you will increase your supporters' commitment to the process. They may even come up with a better idea for how they can help you than the one you had coming into the conversation.

Your initial conversation also sets the tone and the ground rules for your work together. When you perform this step well, you set up effective collaborative relationships with your supporters. When Darrell, The Critic, had this conversation with his supporters, he created relationships that operated in only one direction. Everyone he spoke to had the right to question and challenge his behavior, but he didn't have the right to discuss the situation. He didn't have the right to work with his supporters to evaluate when he should and when he shouldn't be critical. This was a flaw in the set up of his support. The way he set up these relationships, he wasn't an active partner in the change. His only right was to passively listen as his supporters critiqued him.

Of course, it is essential for you to listen to your supporters when they try to help you. Otherwise, you will do what I did when I was in Miami. You will frighten people off and convince them they shouldn't try to help you in the future. If you do not effectively listen, you will show people that you really aren't interested in what they have to say. This will sabotage your whole process, which is why the setup of your relationship is so important. If you set up your supporters to act in ways that will truly help you, then you will be much better able to hear and accept their support. Here is what happened with Susan and her husband.

The Worker

The obvious person to support me was my husband. He lives with me and sees my workaholic behaviors and is affected as much as anyone. So I asked him to work with me throughout the process. He had already helped me understand the importance of making this change for my family and also for me, personally. Then I asked him to help me develop strategies to reduce the time I spent at my office and increase the time I spent with my family. The first strategy that I proposed was for him to tell me when I drifted back to my old habits.

However, it wasn't as simple as that. I knew from past experience that I couldn't tolerate someone "waiting up for me." If he sat by the door and reprimanded me every time I was late getting home from work, it would drive me insane. That just felt too much like my parents waiting for me to come home from a date. If I didn't get home by our agreed time then I got in trouble. It didn't matter if I was five minutes late or two hours late, and it didn't matter if I had been home on time the last 20 times I went out.

So I asked my husband not to point these lapses out to me in the moment when they occurred. I knew there would be times when I would work late. There would be times when I would make business calls when we were at family or social functions. I knew these things would happen, and I knew that I wouldn't respond well to him telling me about it in the moment. This may be unfair to him, but I knew that I would feel like he was pouncing on me and trying to punish me.

Instead, we both agreed to create time once per week to talk about my work. In these discussions we both got to talk about the times that I spent at work and at home. This gave us an opportunity to discuss my record for the past week as well as strategies for the upcoming week. This really helped me feel like we were partners, instead of feeling like he was the judge and jury evaluating me and my crimes.

In the system that Susan and her husband created they made talking about Susan's efforts a lot easier on both of them and also more effective for the change she was trying to make. She recognized how immediate feedback would be counterproductive and created a process that worked for her needs and her husband's needs. Their weekly sessions provided a chance for them to discuss Susan's progress in a way that made both of them comfortable, while still being effective in supporting the change.

When you define your support relationship, you are working with your supporter to clarify her role and the rules for your work together. Your support agreement can be as formal or informal as you wish to make it. You can write it down and sign it, or you can simply discuss it. The important thing for you and your supporter is that the agreement is designed to effectively support your change, and that it is accepted by both of you.

The conversation in which you ask for support and define that support can have a great impact on the effectiveness of that relationship. Following are discussion points that you may wish to consider as you have these discussions with your supporters:

- What ideas do you have for how your supporter can help you make the change?

- How frequently, when, and for how long will you meet/ speak with your supporter? For example, you might say, "We'll talk weekly, on Monday mornings, for the next three months."

- What expectations of confidentiality do you have regarding your change efforts and the conversations you will have with your supporter?

- What other expectations do you have of one another? You might expect your supporter to be honest and fair. Your supporter might expect you to be open and not to judge her for the support she provides.

After asking these questions, it is important to show your appreciation regardless of your supporter's responses to your questions. Saying "thank you" and showing sincere appreciation will go a long way toward making your support relationship more effective.

Exercise 5.2   Define and Seek Support
For each of the supporters you wish to approach, write down the questions you would like to ask and the points you would like to make in the discussion. This is the second half of the discussion guide that you began in the last exercise. Once you have completed both halves of your discussion guide, approach each of your supporters to request their help and define what you are asking of them. Use your discussion guide to ensure that you cover what you intend.

Once you and your supporters have agreed to work together, you will face the next challenge of making that relationship work. Just because someone says they will play a role, doesn't mean that you won't still have to nudge them along to get them to make good on their commitments. Maintaining an effective support relationship simply takes a little attention and appreciation, and that will be the topic of the next chapter.

Maintain Effective Support

Questions to get you started:

What if someone isn't helpful?

How can you keep people excited about supporting your change?

"I've seen a lot of good relationships turn bad." That is what Jasmine explained to me as her rationale for an uncommon practice she uses in business and personal settings. She told me that once a month she asks the question, "How are we doing?" She asks this of key colleagues at work and her husband at home. When she asks this question she isn't looking for sales numbers or a state of the family. She wants to know how her relationship with the person is progressing. She's looking to find out if any obstacles have arisen that might stand in the way of their communication and/or trust.

She told me of a manager she once had who was initially open to feedback and then became more and more defensive over time. She described a friend who had recently gotten a divorce, because she and her husband became incapable of speaking openly about their marriage or their relationship to one another. Neither of these situations started out with poor communication, but they both ended there. To avoid a similar fate, Jasmine adopted the routine of asking, "How are we doing?"

How can you keep your supporters supporting you?

In the last step we discussed how to start a support relationship on the right track. Unfortunately, without some form of maintenance even the strongest foundation can crumble over time. Once you have established your network of supporters, defined the role that each of them will play, and begun your work with them, there are two things you can do to maintain those relationships and keep them operating effectively:

- Solicit feedback in an open and engaging way.
- Adjust your support as needed.

Be Open to Feedback

Some (or all) of your supporters will have the responsibility of providing feedback to you on your behavior. Many people will be uncomfortable with and shy away from giving you critical feedback. They may not believe that you really want to be pushed, or they may be afraid that they'll hurt your feelings if they provide honest feedback. In the workshops I run I ask for feedback several times. I ask my participants to help me make the workshop better for them, and then I ask two questions: "What is working? What would you like to change?"

The first time I ask these questions I always get a handful of responses to the first question and little or no response to the second. By the end of the workshop, I need shorthand to keep up with the comments that all of the participants have, both for what is working and for what to change. The reason that they are so much more open each time I ask is that they become convinced of two things.

First, they realize that I really want to know. I try to convey my interest from the start in how I ask the questions. I don't just blurt out, "What should I change?" I ask them to help me make this a better workshop. I ask them my questions, and then I force them to answer by being patient and allowing for as much silence as they need in order to give a response. I also encourage their responses by consistently thanking them for their input.

Second, they realize that I will act on their suggestions. I don't just ask for feedback on what has already passed in the workshop. Whenever it's appropriate, I ask for suggestions for how I can implement their ideas in the next segment. Then I do my best to implement their ideas immediately and use them throughout the remainder of the workshop. Whether they have commented on the food or the room setup or my presentations or the exercises, I try to make those changes as quickly as possible.

Here's how Karen described her experience with getting feedback from her supporters.

The Pushover

I knew that the people who were most affected by my behavior at work were the people who worked for me. I didn't think that I was going to get much help from my peers or my boss, since they probably loved the fact that I said "yes" to every one of their requests. So I told my team that I was going to work on saying "no." I was going to try to fight more for our team and for their rights. I told each of them to let me know any time they saw me being a pushover.

Then we had a big departmental meeting, and I did it again. Without even thinking I jumped right up to take on a stupid meaningless project. No one said anything to me. At the end of the week I had meetings with everyone on my team. I asked each one of them if they had seen me being a pushover. They had nothing to say. I couldn't believe it.

Then a few more weeks went by. I kept on meeting with them every week, and I kept on asking them, "What have you seen me do? When was I a pushover?" It took a couple of meetings, but they eventually opened up. They started to tell me the things that I had noticed,

and they pointed out things that I hadn't even realized I had done. I
think they weren't really sure at first that I wanted to know. Also, since
I always try to be so nice to people, I think they may have been afraid
that they were going to hurt my feelings. All in all, it takes nerves to tell
your boss that she screwed up, even if she is a pushover.

Karen discovered that when asking for feedback it frequently requires several requests before people will really share their views.
When you bring someone else into your efforts to change, you
need to create a safe environment for them. They need to feel confident that their time and effort will be well spent in helping you
and that their own risk is limited. They need to feel confident that
you really want the support you are asking for and that you will
act on their input. Whether you ask for feedback or for someone
to develop strategies with you or for help in any other way, there is
a simple process you can follow to help you make these conversations effective:

1. Ask
2. Listen
3. Ask
4. Listen
5. Acknowledge
6. Discuss
7. Repeat.

When you ask for your supporter's input, make sure that you
simply ask without providing the answer. I've heard a lot of people
in these situations make statements when they think they are asking
a question. They will say, "What do you think I should change? Because I was thinking that . . ." When asking a question, the simplest
and best strategy is to make it short and then stop.

Stop talking and listen until your supporter speaks. If you can
be comfortable waiting through the silence, your supporter will usually tell you something. If you are really good, you will be quiet some

more. There will frequently be more that your supporter didn't say in her first breath. She would have been perfectly happy not saying more, but if you use silence to your advantage, she will share more of her thoughts.

Then, ask again and listen again. Be willing to entertain the possibility that your supporter has more to say than she revealed after your initial question. Remember that this process is outside of her comfort zone as well as yours. Your willingness and ability to ask and be silent will help you get the most out of your supporters.

Next, acknowledge her. Always say, "thank you." This isn't just for politeness. Your supporter needs to feel appreciated so that she will be eager to continue to help you. These should not be one-time conversations. Rather, you need this relationship to continue. Saying "thank you" is one of the ways you can encourage people to continue to support you.

Once you have received input from your supporter, you may want to discuss it with her. In this discussion you want to explore possibilities to find the best solutions. If your supporter suggests an action you think will be difficult, you may want to ask, "What other alternatives can we come up with?" If she provides you feedback that you behaved poorly, you might ask, "What else could I have done in that situation?" Managing this conversation effectively is important for promoting a productive relationship with your supporter and helping you make valuable changes.

Once you have effectively taken the first six actions, you will need to repeat this process regularly. Repetition of this process will have many benefits. You will become more effective at conducting these conversations. You will get more honesty and openness from your supporters. You will become more committed to your change. You will identify better and better ideas for how to make the change actually happen. Finally, repetition of these conversations will truly surround you with your support network. Your supporters and the conversations you have with them will be your second Circle of Strength that will help you make meaningful and lasting change.

Exercise 6.1　Schedule Your Support

Schedule your meetings with each of your supporters for the next month. Do this in whatever way works best for you. This could include:

• Creating recurring tasks or meetings on your computer or PDA;

• Writing down appointments in your paper organizer or calendar;

• Posting notes on your refrigerator.

Once you have scheduled your appointments, use the process outlined above to make the best use of your time with your supporters.

Consistently engaging your supporters is important for you and your change process. Keep your supporters involved. Keep asking them for their feedback and input, and most important, when they give it to you, be quiet and listen.

Make Adjustments

It is all too easy to ask someone to help you and assume you are done. However, your responsibility will continue on for as long as you need the support. In the end, you are the one who owns your change. You must be the one to ensure that your supporters follow through on their commitments. Some of your supporters will be more helpful than others. Some will need less encouragement than others. It is a mistake to create your support strategy and then assume that it will all go exactly according to plan.

I once worked on a team that experienced phenomenal success, so much so that my company expanded our budget to grow from 4 to 19 people. When we got the approval for this expansion we made all kinds of plans. We designed new strategies for our group and new directions for our clients. Then we designed 15 new roles and hired people into each of them. We had everything planned out to perfection.

The problem was that things didn't turn out to be perfect. When people showed up for the roles that we hired them into, some of them fit and some of them didn't. Some excelled from the start. Some needed more coaching and direction to fully understand how to play their roles. Some needed new roles made for them because they didn't fit the original plans, and some didn't fit any role and had to be let go. No matter how well you set things up and how well you plan, sometimes people do things that don't fit into your design.

The same is true of the supporters you invite into your process. They may or may not take to the role you outlined for them. While it is important to remember that they are doing you a favor, that doesn't mean that they are off limits for you to evaluate. Your change is your responsibility and so is making sure that your supporters are effective in supporting your efforts. Evaluating them doesn't have to be an extensive process, but at the end of each of the first few months of your efforts, ask yourself how everyone is doing. You should be able to place them in one of four categories:

	Interest in helping	
High	**Reset** Doing well but would be more helpful with a little encouragement	**Relax** Doing great; no action necessary
Low	**Release** Shouldn't be one of my supporters	**Redesign** Can definitely help me, but not in this role

Ability to help

Low   High

Interest in helping

Obviously, what you want is lots of people in the Relax category who have shown that they are both capable of and interested in helping you. Then you can simply enjoy and utilize their support. However, not everyone will be like that. Those in the Reset group are people who you know are capable of playing the role but they just don't do it or are inconsistent. They need your encouragement to continue to play the role on a regular basis. You may have other supporters in the Redesign category who are quite enthusiastic about helping you, but they are ineffective at what you asked them to do. Your challenge with them is to discuss new roles that they could play that might fit better with their abilities. Finally, there will be supporters in the Release category. After a while it may become clear to you that they just can't help you. At that point you can either thank them and tell them that you don't need their support or simply stop asking.

Here's how John describes his experience with two of his supporters.

The Talker

I had two coworkers, Cameron and Elizabeth, who I really got wrong. Cameron was supposed to help me by sitting across from me during meetings and tapping his pen when he thought I was talking too much. Elizabeth was supposed to report to me afterwards on how I did. Since we were almost always in the same meetings, I thought they would be perfect people to help me with this. I liked them. I trusted them. They seemed right for the role, but neither of them did what I asked them to do.

Cameron never signaled me during the meetings. Then, after the meetings if I asked him if I talked too much he would give me a rundown of when I had and what I said. At the same time Elizabeth always told me that I was fine. This really confused me at first, but it didn't take long to figure out the pattern. Cameron was highly engaged in our meetings and just wasn't able to focus his attention on me. However, he was great at giving me feedback after the fact. Elizabeth was terrific at bolstering my self-esteem, but she was completely incapable of delivering a tough message.

I had to revamp my approach. Cameron was great at delivering feedback. So I made it my practice to ask him about my behavior after each of our meetings. Unfortunately, I couldn't find an effective role for Elizabeth. So, I just stopped asking her for feedback, and she never brought it up again.

John learned an important lesson that change rarely follows a straight line. It takes trial and error and experimentation with different strategies. Cameron was happy to help John. He showed that by his willingness to provide feedback. Unfortunately, Cameron was also highly engaged in the meetings and wasn't able to focus on helping John in that atmosphere. John needed to redesign Cameron's role to be an informing partner who told him the truth about his behavior in the meetings. Elizabeth was a wonderful person to have as a friend and colleague, but wasn't particularly helpful for John's purposes. In all likelihood, she felt relieved to be released from the responsibility.

You may feel awkward about changing your plans or ending the process with your supporters. However, you are allowed to stop partnering with someone. If you are not getting what you need out of the relationship, you have the right to stop it. Many people feel uncomfortable or guilty over ending a support relationship with someone. The fact is that not everyone will be a good fit for your goals, and this isn't always apparent before you've started the process.

At the same time be careful if it becomes a trend for you that you think your supporters aren't meeting your needs. If this happens once or twice, then you have stood up for your own needs. If it happens three times or more, it may say more about you and your willingness to be helped than it does about any of the people with whom you have partnered.

The other thing to keep in mind is that you will get as much out of these relationships as you put into them. Some people treat their supporters like they do house painters. They want to hire them and come home to a finished product. "Fix me!" they say, but in reality your supporters are more like dance teachers. When you come to class and stand in front of them they listen, observe, and offer what input they can. It is still your responsibility to go to class, talk to the teacher, and do the work between sessions. Those actions are what will determine your results.

Exercise 6.2   Adjust Your Support

Every four weeks or so review your supporters. Ask yourself:

• Are they helping me? Is it in the way that I intended or some other manner?

• Are they willing and/or eager to provide support to me?

• Are they able to provide this support and/or some other kind of support?

Use the chart on page 97 to determine if you need to relax, reset, redesign, or release with each or your supporters. Then take the relevant action with each one.

The Circle of Support

You have now completed your second Circle of Strength. You have surrounded yourself with people who will help you to break your self-addiction. This circle will be around you at all times. The people you chose may live with you or work with you. They may be members of your family or friends or coworkers. The strength of the Circle of Support is its prevalence in your life. You see these people all the time, and your ongoing conversations with them will push you to continuously confront your behavior.

The key is this: stay engaged and maintain the conversation with each of your supporters. Even those people with the best intentions will usually follow your lead. If you ignore or neglect your own efforts for long enough, your supporters will lose interest and stop pushing you. However, if you choose your supporters wisely and give them the right encouragement, you should find that they will be an invaluable source of motivation, information, and energy for you.

Of course, in the end, all of the support and awareness in the world won't change you if you don't act on your own behalf. You need to develop routines to help you prepare for, perform, and evaluate your new behaviors. That is our next topic as we move on to the Circle of Action.

Part III

Taking Action

In this section you will build a Circle of Action, designing steps you can take to reshape your behavior. You will surround yourself with these new routines so that you have clear actions to take before, during and after the moments when your self-addictions surface. Specifically, you will look at the following ways that you can build your Circle of Action:

Step 7: Prepare Yourself
Develop understanding of your new, desired behaviors and build your ability and confidence to perform them in critical moments.

Step 8: Act In the Moment
Design strategies to recognize and stop self-addictive behaviors in the situations in which they are most likely to surface and encourage and facilitate new, more desirable behaviors.

Step 9: Assess Your Progress
Build a routine for regularly assessing your progress toward your goals and recommitting yourself to your efforts.

Raising Awareness

Taking Action

Step 7:
Prepare Yourself

Step 8:
Act in the Moment

Step 9:
Assess Your Progress

Building Support

Circles of Strength

Prepare Yourself

Questions to get you started:

What is the new skill you are trying to master?

How do you prepare yourself for important moments in life?

There is a scene that actors and actresses play out in movies that I am confident you have seen, regardless of your taste in film. They have done it in action movies, comedies, dramas, horror, you name it. It is a scene where the hero is about to do something important and out of the ordinary. Sometimes he needs to have a very important conversation with another character. Sometimes he has to prepare for a big event. What he does in his scene is practice what he is about to perform. Actors who have done this include:

- Robert De Niro in *Taxi Driver*
- Steve Martin in *Dirty Rotten Scoundrels*
- Julie Andrews in *My Fair Lady*
- Ralph Macchio in *The Karate Kid*

- Sylvester Stallone in *Rocky II*
- Annette Bening in *The American President*
- Patrick Swayze in *Ghost*
- Johnny Depp in *Ed Wood*
- Kevin Klein in *Dave*
- Hillary Swank in *Million Dollar Baby.*

In all of these cases these actors were trying to take unnatural actions and make them natural. They practiced speeches, fighting, posture, and manners. Regardless of the skill, these actors repeated their new behaviors over and over. As they practiced, we, as the audience, saw their nervousness grow at first, then eventually dissipate as they neared the triumphant moment.

Our hero's anxiety is raised because he is doing something that is out of the ordinary for him. Maybe he's never asked a girl out before. Maybe he's asked out hundreds, but never one that he really cared about. Maybe he's about to talk to someone more powerful than anyone he's ever met. Regardless of the reason for his anxiety, our hero knows that this situation is too important to leave to chance. So he prepares himself, practicing his words and his actions to build his confidence and his ability for the critical moment.

How can you prepare for action?

In your own critical moments, you too need to be prepared. At these times your most likely response will be the one that is most familiar or comfortable. Martial arts are based on the principle of preparedness. When people learn karate or any other martial art, they practice the same moves over and over and over again. The reason black belts can block a punch or place a kick against an opponent is that they have practiced these moves until they become second nature.

Our natural tendency to take the action that is most familiar to us is one of the reasons self-addictions are so hard to break. If we have performed a given action hundreds or thousands of times in the past, then it will come more readily to us than one that is new and unfamiliar. Despite our best intentions and the desires and support of our friends, family and colleagues, our self-addictions will continue.

The time for you to act is before you ever get in the situations where your self-addiction arises. You need to prepare yourself before your self-addiction takes over. In Step 7 we will examine three ways in which you can prepare yourself to act effectively:

- Clarify the new behavior.
- Practice your new skills.
- Track your actions.

Clarify the New Behavior

Eventually you will reach a point where you will be able to stop your self-addictive behavior. When you get there you will need new behaviors to substitute for the old ones. The first element of preparation is gaining greater understanding of what your options are for these new behaviors. You know what you don't want to do. At this point it is time to clarify what you would like to do instead.

Susan, The Worker, needed to learn how to end her work day effectively so that she could comfortably go home to her family. John, The Talker, needed to learn how to ask questions, listen, and maintain a focus on his audience instead of himself. Karen, The Pushover, needed to learn how to say "no," stand up for herself, and assert her own needs. Darrell, The Critic, needed to learn how to be supportive and positive with people.

The Critic

Obviously, I had to stop myself from being so critical, but I also needed to start being more positive. It wouldn't have been enough for me to eliminate my criticism of people, because that would just leave them in a vacuum, not having any idea what I thought of them. I needed to find a way that I could deliver some positive messages that told people how much I appreciated and respected them. The problem was that I didn't know how to do that without sounding forced or fake.

As a manager, I had been sent to a lot of training programs: "Learn to Lead," "Clear Communication," and "Managing for All," to name a few. I knew that I had been taught about giving positive feedback, but it didn't stick. Whatever I learned about it, I quickly unlearned when I left the class. Certainly it's easy to tell someone, "good job," but I always hated getting those pats on the back. They always sounded too phony to me, and I didn't want the people in my life, at work and at home, to feel like I was feeding them a line.

So I started to read. There were a couple of books that were interesting, but one really gave me what I needed. It offered me a simple process for looking someone in the eye and telling them what they did right. That was what I needed, something that was direct and to the point. I didn't want anything too soft or too vague. It also gave me the reminder I needed—you can't praise someone effectively if you haven't paid enough attention to see them doing something right. This really clarified for me what I needed to do.

Darrell used a book to determine his model of good behavior, but there are many ways to define your new behavior. Writing down your own definition of good behavior is an excellent first step. After all, you might already hold the answer within you. You may be the best resource to design your new actions. Perhaps you have a very clear idea of what actions you want to take, but you've always had difficulty implementing those new behaviors. Now is the time to combine the lessons of this book with whatever model of good behavior you have.

Once you have identified your own views on the topic, you can look at what other sources have to say. As you research what other people recommend, look for new ways of acting that fit your personal style. You might try going to your local bookstore and looking for a book on your topic. Chances are good that someone else has already thought quite a bit about whatever it is that you are trying to change and has written a book. It is a good time to sit down in your bookstore and take advantage of the fact that many other people have probably faced problems similar to your own. It could be a book on diet or fitness, anger management or delegation, organization or self-respect. Whatever your self-addiction, there is almost certainly someone who has developed a model of good behavior to match it.

There are options besides looking at your own knowledge or reading a book to build your expertise. There are experts and gurus for just about any behavior you want to change. They write books and magazine articles and they offer workshops that provide you with a wealth of information for what good behavior looks like. You can almost certainly find websites that will offer advice on any subject. However, there are many sources of misinformation on the Internet. So beware if that is the direction you choose. Your goal here is to define clearly and in detail what specific behaviors you wish to adopt.

Exercise 7.1   Find Your Model
Using your own understanding, books you have read, and/or other sources of information that you trust, define and record in your notebook your own definition of good behavior that you will use as an alternative to your self-addiction. Specifically, identify the particular behaviors that you will begin to use going forward.

Practice Your New Skill

If you know what you want to do, why can't you just make it happen? I ask myself this question all the time. One of my great passions in life is basketball. I love to watch it, but nothing compares with playing. The combination of physical challenge and mental concentration create for me what I can only describe as a kind of timelessness. When I am on the court, everything else in the world fades away, and I feel completely in the zone.

By this I don't mean that I am a great basketball player. "In the zone" is a term used a lot in sports to refer to someone who is performing extremely well. This is not the "in the zone" experience that I have. When I am at my best, my play is acceptable, but at my worst I'm less than mediocre. It's not that I don't know how to play or what to do. I know what I *want* to do, and have even visualized myself doing it, but I can't make it happen. I can't make myself play well in the game, because my body doesn't know how to do what my mind tells it.

I can't do what I want to do because desire doesn't lead to execution. Practice and preparation lead to execution. I can't shoot the ball the way I'd like to because the only time I really try to do that is during the game. When I try it during the game I get one chance, and then I might not get another chance to try the same shot again. Besides my lack of practice, I have a lack of understanding. I have a notion of what it takes to shoot a basketball from watching the game on TV, but I've never bothered to learn the fundamentals. Where should my elbow go? When should I release the ball? Where should my off hand be?

New or unnatural behaviors are more difficult to perform, and as our stress levels increase we are more likely to revert to our old behaviors. However, the more prepared we are, the more easily our new behaviors will come to us. Preparing yourself is something that you can do on your own, but is also a great opportunity for you to work with one of the partners you created in the last section. This is a time for you to challenge yourself to see just how prepared you can be.

I recently had a conversation with someone who told me he really wanted to work on asking more questions. He thought that people leaned on him way too much because he would always jump in and provide the answers whenever anyone brought a challenge to him. He thought that if he could get them talking, then the people in his life would start to take responsibility for their own problems. I thought that was a great idea for him. So I asked him, "What are you going to do?"

He said to me, "I'm going to ask more questions."

I said, "Great. Like what?"

He said, "What do you mean?"

He assumed that understanding the value of the questions was enough. Instead, we talked about figuring out and preparing specific questions ahead of time. Some of these were generic and could be used in any conversation:

- Can you tell me more about the situation?

- What have you already tried?

- What are some of your options at this point?

- Who do you know who has gone through something similar?

- What have you done in similar situations in the past?

- What do you think you should do next?

Once he understood how much more he could prepare himself, he wrote down his favorite questions on a card, laminated it, and carried it around with him so that he could refer to it at any time. These were his all-purpose questions that he could use whenever someone put him on the spot.

Next we looked at how he could prepare himself better for the conversations that he knew he would have on any given day. He decided to block out time at the beginning of every day to identify specific questions that he would ask in the meetings or conversations that he knew he would have that day. These preparation strategies helped him to more easily perform his new behaviors. That's also what happened with Karen.

The Pushover

If only it were easy to just say "no." When I'm put on the spot, it doesn't matter what I think or what I want. It's like my brain no longer controls my mouth. I just have to sit back and watch as my mouth says, "yes," to whatever request comes along. In order to break this routine I decided that I needed to slow down these conversations. Part of my bad habit was that I would always say "yes" to people without even knowing what I was agreeing to. Even when I did understand, I never gave myself time to think things through before giving in.

I started with the idea that I might be better at standing up for myself if I could delay some of my responses. So I prepared some questions that I could ask people when they put me on the spot. I would ask, "What exactly are you asking for?" And I would ask at least one more follow-up question based on the answer I got. Then I would say, "Let me think about it." This was important both for giving me more time and for giving me more control.

I also made a list of the things I had agreed to that I most resented afterwards. At first I was tempted to blame the people who asked for these things, but I realized that I needed to take responsibility. I'm the one who offered to do them. Still, knowing what created resentment helped me to prepare myself to respond to other requests down the line. I actually developed a mantra that I repeated to myself to avoid committing to things I would resent later on.

My mantra was, "What I want matters." This reminded me that I was allowed to have needs and desires, too. Specifically, this prepared and prompted me to evaluate my own wants whenever I had to decide whether or not to do something. I would rate the task on a scale of one to ten on whether or not I wanted to do it. The ones were like the list I made of things that I resented afterwards. The tens were things that I absolutely loved to do. Between five and four they crossed a line between what I was willing to do and things that I would resent if I said "yes."

I don't have to love everything I agree to do, but I also shouldn't do things that make me angry with myself and the person I'm helping. That's what my resentment did to me. That had to change. I need to be responsible to other people, but I also need to be responsible to myself.

Karen's mantra and rating system helped her be prepared to use her new behaviors. The better prepared you are, the easier it will be to break out of your usual routines and enact your new, desired behaviors. In Step 5 you prepared scripts to guide you through the process of asking for support. In the upcoming activity you will prepare the scripts or questions or statements that you will use to create your new behavior patterns. What you create will depend on your specific self-addiction as you can see from our four examples:

- Karen, The Pushover, developed specific questions and a mantra. These helped her to slow down her decision making process and to be aware of her own needs.

- John, The Talker, defined questions and statements to deflect the conversation away from him. This created space for other people to speak.

- Darrell, The Critic, prepared and practiced comments of praise. He also prepared questions to get others talking about their perceptions of what was working and what wasn't. That way he had an alternative to jumping in with his criticism.

- Susan, The Worker, developed a set of questions to ask herself at 3:00 every day. These helped her put her work and family obligations in perspective when there was still time left in the workday to allow her to make needed adjustments and get home at a reasonable time.

As you can see, your preparation could be directed towards meetings with others or time for yourself. You could prepare statements or questions to speak aloud or mantras to speak silently and to drive your thinking. Whatever the case may be, your goal is to write down what you will do when you reach the moment of action.

Exercise 7.2   Mark Your Words
Follow these two steps to prepare yourself to engage in your desired behavior: • Write down the questions and/or statements you wish to use and when you wish to use them. • Read what you wrote down at least twice each day for 10 days.

The prepared words will give you certainty about what you want to say. Rereading them will build your confidence in delivering the words and will develop a new circle to keep you coming back to your commitment.

If your self-addiction—criticizing, interrupting, not listening, for example—shows up during conversations, then it might be even more challenging to use your new behavior effectively in the moment. For these self-addictions, role-playing is a great way to get ready for the real event. To practice with a supporter, start by identifying a situation that is likely to bring on your addictive behaviors. Then have your supporter play the role of the person who will trigger these bad behaviors, and practice having a conversation with him. Coach your supporter on how to act to make it as true to life as possible.

You can also prepare by yourself by acting out the situation and pretending that the person who brings out your self-addiction is in the room with you. The time you spend in your car is a great time to practice your new behaviors. Think of yourself like one of the characters in the movies mentioned at the start of this chapter. You need to rehearse your new behavior in order to get it right when the important moment arrives.

Track Your Actions

Great performers of all types, including athletes, singers, and actors, know that the best way to improve performance is to learn from past experience. They do this by watching recordings of themselves in action and/or reviewing their performance with observers such as directors and coaches. Maybe they discover that they start off slowly or that they hit a lull before intermission. Maybe the audience has a strong effect on their actions. They learn when their performance was exceptional and when it was below standard. By reviewing their performance they gain an opportunity to make adjustments and improve.

Keeping track of your actions means observing and writing down three things:

- Any time you engage in your self-addictive behavior
- Any time you engage in the replacement behaviors you defined earlier in this chapter
- What caused each of the above.

You probably won't have the luxury of having a running video camera during those times when your self-addictions flare up. However, that doesn't mean that you can't review what you've done. Susan, The Worker, found a way to evaluate her actions.

The Worker

I started keeping a daily log of the hours I spent at work. I wrote down what time I was in my office and when I took calls or worked from home. I kept a record of all of the work I did. By looking at my log, it was easy to tell when I was working more or less on which days or in what weeks, but it wasn't clear why.

The next step for me was to look at what I was working on. I didn't do this for everything I did during the regular work week. What I recorded was the work that I did outside of normal business hours. If I stayed at the office until 9 PM, then I recorded what I did from 6-9. If I made calls on the weekend, then I wrote down what they were about. Still, this didn't help me see any pattern.

Then I looked at it one other way. I started to write down what was happening in my personal life when my work went into overdrive. What was going on with my husband or my kids? This provided the key, and it was remarkable how clear it was. I always worked hard, but there was a clear cause for when I worked the hardest. That happened whenever there was something important happening in my family life. If I had a terrific night with my husband or if we got in a fight, I was sure to work late the next day. When we first discussed that our son was of an age that we should have a talk with him about sex and drugs, I worked late every night for a week.

It was as though my work was a shield that I held out to protect myself from being too close to my family. It stopped me from having to work too hard at being a good wife and mother. It made it so that if I failed at either one, it wouldn't be my fault. I would have work as my excuse.

The truth is, if I don't work as many hours, it forces me to be more effective in the time that I do work. If I can't bill as many hours, that's not going to bankrupt either my law firm or my family. I wasn't working so hard because the work demanded it. I was working so hard because it allowed me to avoid things at home that I didn't want to confront.

Keeping a list enabled Susan to discover what caused her workaholic behavior. The key is to consistently track your self-addictive behavior and your replacement behavior. Then, in order to get at what caused each, ask yourself questions like:

- When did the behavior occur?
- Who was involved?
- What sparked it?

Observing your behaviors will give you an understanding of what people or things in your environment facilitate your self-addictive behaviors. Recognizing these patterns will help you to better prepare yourself. You will be able to look out for certain situations and change your strategies based on what your environment is throwing your way. For Susan that means that she needs to increase her focus on her commitments when there are significant events going on in her family life.

Keeping a running list of your actions will also bring your awareness up to the moment of action. The moment of action is when you have a choice of how to act. When most people decide that they want to change their behavior, they do so during some time of reflection. Unfortunately, recognizing your behavior during reflection is very different from recognizing it in the moment. What you can do in the moment will be discussed in more detail in Step 8, Act In the Moment. For now, it is important to recognize that the list you keep will bring your awareness up to the moment of action.

Keeping lists will help you gain heightened awareness by giving you a way to consistently focus on your actions. If you know that you need to record your actions every day, then they will remain at the forefront of your mind. The more frequently and consistently you sit down to review your actions the more you will increase your awareness of those actions. These reviews can also all be done in only a few minutes per day. For example:

- Darrell sat down for five minutes at the end of every day and wrote down what compliments and what criticisms he had dispensed. At the end of each week he reviewed his list to look for patterns.

- Karen also spent five minutes at the end of her day writing down any requests she had heard that day and what her response was to each one.

By adding to your list every day, you are building a routine that creates a Circle of Action. This is one more way that you surround yourself with your change effort. It is not a one-time action or event. Rather, it is a circular process with many repetitions. This consistency is valuable in identifying the patterns of your behaviors. At least once each day you should be evaluating your behavior and recording your observations. The more consistently you observe yourself, the more you will be able to recognize the patterns in your life and the more quickly you will raise your self-awareness.

Exercise 7.3   Track Your Behavior

At least once per day write down any instances when you engaged in either your self-addictive behavior or your replacement behavior. Once per week review your observations and answer the following questions:

- When did I engage in the behavior?
- Who was involved?
- What happened beforehand that caused my response?
- When did my self-addictive and replacement behaviors happen the most?

Make sure to keep these observations on a consistent basis.

These actions can dramatically alter your awareness of your behavior and your ability to act in the moment, but consistency is the key. If you only record these observations once per week, you will lose sight of many of the times that you engage in your behavior. It will not be at the forefront of your mind, and your awareness will not reach the moment of action. However, if you even spend just a few minutes per day recording your observations, you will take a big step toward breaking your self-addiction.

Surrounding With Action

When you prepare yourself for action, you take the necessary steps to make success easier to achieve. You should know what good behavior looks like, what specific words you want to speak and/or actions you want to take to begin your new behaviors, and when you are most at risk of falling into your old behaviors. All of this preparation serves to raise your awareness and remake your environment to surround yourself with new cues for positive action. In Step 8, Act In the Moment, we will examine the actions you can take and patterns you can create to surround yourself with more positive cues when you arrive at the moment of action.

Act In the Moment

Questions to get you started:

How will you realize that the
moment to act has arrived?

Who will decide your actions, you
or your self-addiction?

Two months after I quit my job to create my own consulting company, I heard a speaker deliver a presentation on how people who
start their own businesses need to be a little bit crazy. I found him
entertaining and insightful, but I didn't realize how on target he was
at the time. After a couple of years in business it was much clearer to
me just how crazy people have to be to succeed as entrepreneurs. As
the owner of a business there is no stability. There always seems to
be either too much work, or too little. Busy is definitely better than
bored, but sometimes it can be extreme.

I remember one time in particular when I felt as though all the
opportunities I had been hoping for hit at the same time. All of a
sudden I had a ton of work to do and no time to do it. I discussed
my situation with a friend, and he helped me develop strategies to
keep me focused and avoid the distractions that could eat away at

my time. It was a very useful conversation. It helped me feel like I could make it through the busy time and lowered my stress level considerably. One of our strategies was that I wouldn't spend time on the Internet during the day unless it was for research into one of my client projects. All of the news that I usually read online would have to wait for the end of the day.

When I got off the phone with my friend I did two things. I checked my email to see if anything critical had come in while I was on the phone, and I opened up my Internet browser. It was true insanity. Only minutes after discussing how I needed to avoid the Internet, I hopped right on. I knew it was wrong. I knew I shouldn't do it, but somehow my brain stood back and watched as my hand guided the mouse to this action. The moment for me to change my behavior had arrived, and I failed my first test. Fortunately, I did figure out a way to stop getting distracted from my work, but it was clear that changing in the moment was not as easy as my friend and I had made it out to be.

What can you do to improve in the moment?

A lot of people credit willpower for their success or failure in these circumstances. I spoke to a woman named Joan recently who was trying to lose weight and expressed frustration over setbacks to her diet program. She worked in a training department, so she was always going to corporate training events. These events carried with them several certainties:

1. The meeting rooms would be sterile and cold.
2. The participants would include a handful who didn't want to be there and would give the trainers a hard time.
3. There would be donuts and Danish pastries at breakfast, cookies and brownies in the afternoon, and soda and coffee all day long.

She had just come back from a week of these events and had gorged herself on all of the fattening foods available to her. It made her feel awful, but she did it anyway. The food just tasted too good at the time. I asked her what she thought she needed to do differently and she told me that next time she really needed to set her mind to the task, to just commit to having willpower.

It is a common belief about change that willpower is what makes the difference. People think, "If only I have the willpower, I can do better in the future." Willpower is great, but in many cases it doesn't hold the key to success. With all of the work you have done to this point, it is too much of a risk to leave the final actions to a test of willpower. In this chapter we will build:

- Understanding of the process of change in the moment of action

- Strategies you can use in the moment of action to shape your new behaviors.

Process of Change

When you reach the time when your self-addictions usually take over, you might have three different experiences in that moment:

- Recognition—Recognizing the self-addiction as you perform it but being unable to stop yourself from doing it.

- Recovery—Realizing you are engaged in the self-addiction and recovering to stop yourself during the act.

- Replacement—Recognizing the desire to engage in the self-addiction and replacing it with a favorable alternative before the behavior begins.

Understanding these three experiences will help you to navigate through them more effectively.

Recognition

There will come a time when you recognize in the moment that you are engaging in the addictive behavior. You might start to perform the undesirable behavior, realize that you are doing it, but be unable to stop yourself. If that happens then it means that your self-control has not yet caught up with your self-awareness. Your awareness has risen to where you recognize the behavior during the event. However, your self-control is not up to the speed of your self-awareness, so the behavior continues.

When you experience awareness without control, rationalization and emotion are generally the key drivers. Rationalization takes place when we recognize the mistakes we are making but figure out some reason that this exact moment is not the best time to make the change. Perhaps we decide that Monday is a better day to start a new routine, or maybe we convince ourselves that this situation isn't *exactly* what we had in mind when we made the commitment. Somehow, we satisfy ourselves that there are perfectly adequate reasons why we don't need to start now.

Emotional causes are very different from rationalization. When emotion drives our behaviors we may have 100% conviction that we should not do what we are doing, but our emotions simply take over. It could be anger, fear, even joy that drives us. Some people even describe this as a near out-of-body experience. It's as though we are observers with little or no control over our own behaviors. We know that what we are doing is wrong. We know we should be doing something else, but we are simply incapable of altering our behavior. That's what used to happen with John.

The Talker

When I tried to make this change, my first attempts were universally unsuccessful. I would be in a meeting trying to make a point and all of a sudden I would realize that I had been talking for a while. So I would try to wrap up my comments, but then I would think that the way I wrapped up didn't make sense. Then I would try to clarify and realize I was going on even longer. So I would just stop, but then someone would say something that made me feel like I hadn't made my point. Then I would jump in again.

The whole time this was happening, my mind was telling me to stop. I would silently shout at myself to just shut up, but I had absolutely no control over myself. It felt like every single thing that someone else

said triggered an idea or a story that I just had to get out. I watched
myself doing this, but most of the time I was powerless to stop. I think
I was like everyone else in the room, just one more annoyed listener
wondering when my speech was going to end.

John knew that he was in the moment of action. He knew it was
time to change his behavior, and he was motivated to do so. Unfortunately, willpower alone wasn't enabling him to change. However,
he had reached the critical first step. Even though he wasn't able to
change that time, he was experiencing recognition of his behavior
in the moment. This recognition is an important stepping-stone to
reach in order to get to recovery.

Recovery

In recovery you adjust in the middle of the act. You recognize the
behavior as you are doing it, and you stop in the middle of your
action to replace the undesirable behavior with the desirable substitute. This is a watershed moment. You have finally engaged in the
behavior that you want to use. Your change now starts to feel real.
Others may not yet realize it, but you have undergone a tremendous
change and can see it taking place.

When you achieve your first recovery it is a terrific moment and
one that you should be thrilled with and celebrate. Unfortunately, it
can also be a time when many change efforts derail. Often these first
attempts at new behaviors are awkward and ineffective and all too
easy to give up. A friend of mine went through this early in her career.
She was very well spoken but timid in groups. Her timidity was a behavior that she wanted to change because she thought it was holding
her back from being recognized by senior management, exposed to
broader opportunities, and promoted into a management role.

Then she found herself in a meeting at work and realized that
she had just passed up an opportunity to speak on an issue she
felt strongly about. She was frustrated and chose to step out of her
comfort zone. She jumped into the conversation and voiced her
opinion on the next topic. Unfortunately, her idea was rejected. No

one recognized or reinforced her effort to engage in new actions. Instead of celebrating the accomplishment of voicing her opinion, she felt dejected and lost her commitment to develop her new behavior. Her self-addiction to avoiding the fray and staying out of the way reasserted itself and came back stronger than ever.

At these times, it is critical to recognize the success of the situation. Focus on the progress that has been made and the opportunity and the benefits that still lie ahead. Others may not yet realize that you have changed, but you can still cheer yourself on and take pride in your accomplishments. Most importantly, you can recommit yourself to continuing your change effort.

Replacement

During replacement you stop yourself from even beginning to exhibit the undesirable behavior. You recognize the situation as one where you might do the wrong thing, and you do the right thing instead. There isn't even a glimmer of the old behavior. What a fantastic change. This feels great! It is also a time to slow down and hold onto the things that brought you your success.

I have a friend named Alison who loves to play pool. When we play together she always says the same thing when one of us gets on a hot streak. She says, "speed kills." What she means is that going too fast can break your streak. Her saying goes for when you take your shot too quickly, not taking the time to set up properly. It also goes for hitting the cue ball too hard, creating unexpected ricochets. She says this during the hot streaks because when we get on a roll, we get excited. Our success goes to our heads. We start to take shortcuts. In effect, we go to all of our bad habits because we are too excited to contain ourselves.

The same lesson applies when you replace your old behavior. It is a wonderful time to celebrate your success and feel great about your accomplishment. It is also a very important time to remind yourself of what you did to create that success and recommit to those actions.

Strategies to Shape Your Behavior

The progression from Recognition to Recovery to Replacement is caused by a combination of awareness and preparation. The observation lists discussed in Step 7 help to bring your awareness up to the moment of action. Once that happens you need skills and strategies that you can use to recover from your self-addictive behavior and eventually replace it.

Replacing an old behavior with a new one is not simply a matter of will. If that were the case, then Joan, the dieter I mentioned earlier in this chapter, would be successful if she committed to trying harder. She was at the stage of Recognition. She knew she shouldn't grab the donuts in the moment, but she did it anyway. The key to changing your behavior in the moment is to create a situation that facilitates your desirable behavior.

That's what we did with Joan. We created a favorable situation for her by changing her actions and her physical environment. We gave her more control by making the desirable behavior easier and the undesirable behavior more difficult to perform. Whenever she was at a training event in the past, she would socialize with the participants. The problem was that the place where they tended to congregate was next to all of the food. When she was right next to the food it became too easy for her to simply reach over and grab a brownie.

When we discussed the situation though, we recognized that not everyone went to the food during breaks. There were almost always people who stayed at their tables or who went out to the hallway to stretch their legs. So she created a new plan of action. Every time there was a break she would target someone who was far away from the food table and engage them in a conversation. She essentially created a new objective for herself. Instead of trying to keep to her diet, her goal was to speak with someone who was a certain distance from the food table. By creating physical distance between herself and the food she gained control over her behavior.

I did something similar to curb my own Internet use that I described at the beginning of this chapter. I simply erased all of the shortcuts that I had on my computer to access the Internet. I used to have shortcuts on my desktop and on the toolbar at the bottom of my screen. No matter what I was doing, I could always see that Internet icon staring at me. As soon as I got frustrated with anything in my work, that icon would draw me in. Erasing these shortcuts did two things. First, it took away the visual temptation. Second, it made it so that I couldn't simply click onto the Internet without thinking. I had to actually go through my start menu and find the program out of a long list of options.

When you try to gain control in the moment, you need to find ways to make the self-addictive behavior difficult to perform and the replacement behavior easy to perform. You can do this by altering your environment to take away the cues that support the self-addiction and by altering your actions to make your replacement behaviors easier to perform.

Let's look at how John, Susan, and Darrell each did this.

The Talker

I started keeping a speaking tally in every meeting I attended. I identified two people in each meeting to watch: one who I considered a quiet type and one who was a talker. Then I kept a tally of every time one of them spoke and every time I spoke. I would mark it down so that I had a running count for each of us. At first I only allowed myself to speak as many times as the quiet person spoke. If he spoke five times during the hour, then I got to open my mouth five times. After awhile I allowed myself a little more freedom, but I always wanted to stay midway between the quiet person and the talker.

This helped me in a couple of ways. First, it gave me something to do. Before I used to spend the whole meeting figuring out what I could say. If I didn't speak, I would get bored. This gave me something to focus my attention on while I wasn't speaking. I actually became a student, studying the interpersonal dynamics of who spoke and who didn't. I started asking myself questions about when certain people spoke up and why. All of this made it easier for me to talk less because my mind had something else to focus on besides speaking.

Second, it forced me to be much more thoughtful about when I would speak up and what I would say. Reducing the number of times I spoke actually cut down the length of my speaking. Since I had to think through my comments, they came out much more directed.

The Worker

I was getting better at leaving the office at a reasonable time. However, I still had the issue of taking my work home with me. The big problem was my Blackberry. Nights, weekends, it was always buzzing. If someone called when I was doing something with my family, I'd excuse myself to answer the call. If an email came in when I was with my kids, I'd reply right away or call the person who sent it.

I convinced myself that I always needed to be connected, but that really wasn't true. I occasionally went to a show with my husband or to a movie with the family. At those times I turned it off. I even went on a weekend bicycle vacation once. We biked during the day and stayed at beautiful country inns at night, and I only used my Blackberry in the morning before the ride started and in the afternoon after the end of the ride. So it was possible for me to disengage, it just wasn't comfortable.

The problem was that my Blackberry was always there. I carried it from room to room all over my house. So I made two changes. I made my bedroom "The Blackberry Room," and I always kept my Blackberry on silent mode. The Blackberry Room was the only room in the house that the Blackberry was allowed. As soon as I came home, I had to deposit it into its room. If I wanted to check my emails or voicemails, I had to go upstairs to The Blackberry Room to do it.

At first I ran up every ten minutes to check, but that became a real pain. Slowly I just checked it less and less. You know what? Nothing happened. No one freaked out that it took me one or two or four hours to respond to something on the weekend. This also helped me when I was out of the house. I knew that if the Blackberry buzzed and it was work related, I could simply let it go until I finished what I was doing. This didn't happen overnight, but I gradually became more and more comfortable with letting work go when I was with my family.

The Critic

I wanted constant reminders to be more positive with people. So I put sticky notes on my computer and my desk. After about two hours they didn't have any impact. They became just that much more clutter and annoyance in my work area. My brain tuned it out. I used to live next to railroad tracks. When friends came over and a train went by they would always ask me how I could stand the noise. I always asked them, "What noise?" When something is always there in the background, your brain just ignores it.

I needed something that was more in my face. I actually ordered new notepads with the question, "What's working?" at the top of each page. While I was waiting for them to arrive I decided that I would just write those two words down before each meeting I had. I always had my notebook with me, and this took all of three seconds. It really changed my mindset.

Sometimes it was just a helpful reminder to stay positive. Sometimes I actually used that question to start my conversations. This was so useful that I gave the notepads away when they arrived and continued the practice of writing down the question at the beginning of every conversation.

In each of these cases some action was taken to either make the addictive behavior more difficult to perform or the replacement behavior easier to carry out. John's tallying other people's comments gave him something to concentrate on besides talking and therefore made it easier for him to remain silent for longer periods of time. Susan made it difficult to check her Blackberry by keeping it far away from herself while she was at home. Darrell's action of writing down, "What's working?" made it easier for him to start his conversations on a positive note and keep his positive frame of mind throughout the discussions.

Water will follow the easiest path downhill. For the most part, our behaviors are the same. We will do that which is easiest, or most natural, or most comfortable. That is usually going to be a repetition of the behavior that we have performed most frequently in the past. That is why our self-addictions persist. They are the easiest paths for us. In the next exercise you will attempt to do what John, Susan and Darrell did. You will look for ways to make your desired actions easier and your self-addictions more difficult to perform.

There are four different cues to be aware of when attempting to shape your behavior:

- **Instigators**—These are the cues that set off your self-addictive behavior. You may have identified some of these when you tracked your behavior in Step 7. The Internet icon on my computer was an instigator for me.

- **Blockers**—These are any factors that stop you from performing the desired new behavior. They could be things in your environment, circumstances in your interactions with others, or people who pull you away from your desired behavior. The participants who congregated at the food table were blockers for Joan, the Dieter.

- **Starters**—These are the specific cues or processes that get you to start the desired activity. For Darrell it was his practice of writing down, "What's working?" These can be alarms or rituals or any kind of cue that reminds you and gets you focused to perform your desired behavior.

- **Green Lights**—These are positive reinforcements or rewards that you get for your desired behaviors. They could be a friend saying, "Great job." They could come from your supporters or from your environment, or they could be things that you do for yourself to reward your good behavior.

The next exercise is your opportunity to create barriers to your undesirable behaviors and cues to support your new behaviors. Now is the time to create specific strategies to change your behavior in the moment.

> ### Exercise 8.1   Shape Your Actions
>
> Identify the Instigators, Blockers, Starters, and Green Lights that currently exist in your environment, then brainstorm as many answers as possible to the following questions:
>
> - How can I minimize or eliminate the Instigators and Blockers?
> - What new Starters and Green Lights can I create to support my new behavior?
>
> When you have answered these questions, identify the strategies that you will employ. Don't overwhelm yourself with too many things to do. Quality is better than quantity. Start with a few key strategies. You can always come back and add more.

Impulses vs. Intentions

Whenever we try to change a behavior, we provoke a fight. We create a struggle between our impulses and our intentions. Our self-addictions represent our impulses trying to maintain the status quo and continue what is most comfortable, regardless of the impact on us. Our desire to change represents our intentions, the clear underdog in this fight, despite the positive benefits we might gain. The question is, "Who will win this fight?"

Whether our impulses or our intentions win will in large part be determined by who and what helps each side. Our impulses have history, the path of least resistance, and environmental cues on their side. Our intentions need a lot of help to tip the scales in their favor. In this chapter you are creating very specific, actionable strategies and changes to your environment to support your intentions. If your impulses occasionally win a victory, don't despair. When you attempt to break a self-addiction you will rarely follow a direct path. You will have both victories and setbacks along the way. You've put in a great effort to this point. Keep going with it and the victories will come more and more often.

In the very beginning of this book we said that self-addictions are incredibly strong. You need to surround yourself with as many different sources of strength as possible in order to break your addictions. In the Circle of Action you have surrounded yourself with rituals and routines and changes to your environment, all to build strength around your new behaviors. There is one more routine, one more action that will give you the final strength you need. We have talked at length about making a change to your behavior. In the next chapter we will talk about actions you can take to recover from any setbacks you experience and sustain the changes you make over time.

Assess Your Progress

Questions to get you started:

How are you doing on your commitments?

What has facilitated or inhibited your efforts?

What is your next commitment?

I always ask my clients to make commitments. At the beginning of our work together we outline major goals for the next several months. At the end of each session, we work together to determine specific actions they will take before their next session. I had one client who was adamant at the beginning of almost every session that she had so much to discuss, so much ground to cover with me, that there was no time to go over what she had or hadn't done relative to her commitments. It was early in my career, and not knowing any better at the time, I followed her lead.

So each time we talked, we would discuss new developments in her work. To be fair, she did always come prepared with very interesting new challenges to discuss. Sometimes these related to her central goals for the coaching, but more often than not, these conversations would lead in completely new directions. The discussions were fast paced and varied, and at the end of our work together she described the coaching as generally helpful to her. However, both she and her manager were disappointed that the coaching had failed to help her achieve her original goals.

I felt awful. I thought that I had been doing a great job and that all of the commitments along the way would create success. After all, she had clearly defined goals, and there were always specific action items that came out of our conversations, some of which directly affected her goals. I figured that I had done everything right. Unfortunately, I left out one key action. I never pushed her to review her progress.

What should you do to assess your progress?

It is tempting to believe at this point that everything will work out. If you have followed the recommendations in this book, then you have put a great deal of work into achieving your desired change. You should be optimistic that you will succeed with all of the effort you have put into this process. However, regardless of the amount of effort or thoroughness you have put in up to this point, there are four important reasons for you to assess your progress:

- To catch your relapses
- To recommit
- To make things easier
- To sustain your change.

Catch Your Relapses

Relapse can and will happen. It's a natural part of the process. It's your mind's attempt to return to comfortable patterns, especially before the new routines have been firmly established. The important question isn't whether you will relapse. It's, "What happens when the relapse occurs?" Success and relapse are not mutually exclusive when breaking self-addictions. Relapse is simply part of the journey. How you deal with relapse will determine your ultimate ability to succeed.

When people think about relapse with drugs and alcohol, images arise of the addict binging on his old vice and falling hard off the wagon. However, with self-addictions relapses are far subtler. The difference is that there is no clear break the way there is with alcohol or drugs. If someone is an alcoholic and takes a drink, it is clear they have broken their sobriety. If someone has a self-addiction to controlling behavior and tells someone else what to do, it isn't clear what they have done. Did they relapse to their old behaviors? Or were they merely acting appropriately given the circumstances? What if Susan, The Worker, works late one night? Has she relapsed? Or was she responding properly to the demands of her job? The subjective nature of self-addiction is what makes it so important to watch for relapses and assess your progress along the way.

The Talker

I kept daily and weekly scorecards for myself. They weren't elaborate. At the end of each day I rated myself on a scale of one to ten on how I had done in sharing the conversations. I gave separate ratings for group and one-on-one meetings. Then, at the end of the week, I would look at the scores and track my progress over time. I used this process to keep me focused on my goals and to catch myself if I slipped. I also used input from friends and colleagues to guide my scoring.

I found that I did pretty well for a while. Then my scores slipped when some of my old behaviors returned, particularly in one-on-one conversations. I started out making a point of asking at least three questions at the beginning of any discussion before I launched into any stories of my own. Then, as I got better at sharing the dialogue with others, I gradually began to loosen up on my three question requirement and be more natural about it. My friends and coworkers noticed that I started to dominate the discussions a little and dropped their scores. It wasn't major, but it was a dip back toward my old behavior and a helpful reminder to be vigilant.

Then I got another, more serious reminder. I was feeling a little stressed over a project that I was working on, and stress definitely brings out my talking. One of my friends at work stopped by my office and asked me if I had heard the news about one of our coworkers. It turned out that he had been diagnosed with cancer and was telling people because he was going to miss some time at work in order to get treatment. I felt really bad for him and went right over to see him to express my concern and support.

When I did my nightly scorecard it occurred to me that I had spoken with that person before I heard the news from my friend. I wondered why he wouldn't have told me himself. Then I replayed the conversation in my mind. Sure enough, I had done more than just slip a little. I had had a full-blown return to my old behaviors. I let my anxiety send my mouth into overdrive. It must have been ten or fifteen minutes into the discussion, or maybe I should say monologue, before I finally asked him what was new in his life. He must have been too exhausted or aggravated at that point to tell me.

John's routine for reviewing his actions gave him the information he needed to catch his relapse. Review routines are important because it is almost a certainty that you will slip back into your old behaviors at some point. If you have no routine to monitor your progress, your relapse may very well go unnoticed. It is all too easy to slide into your old behavior patterns without even noticing. Setting up a routine to evaluate your progress will help you identify when these slips occur and help you to return to your new, desired behaviors.

Recommit

In Step 3, Making Powerful Commitments, I suggested that you should make commitments that were achievable and of short duration. These are more manageable and give you an opportunity to ex-

---

Exercise 9.1   Catch Your Relapse

Answer the following questions to determine how you will catch yourself:

- What will I do each day to track my actions?

- What will I do each week to evaluate my progress?

- Who else will I ask for input? When will I ask for this input?

Once you have answered the questions above, be sure to schedule time in your calendar for your daily and weekly review activities and/or leave yourself reminders to complete these actions.

---

perience success. However, they are only truly valuable if you have a process to recommit. It does you little good to make a minor change to your behavior or change for a month and then return to all of your old behaviors immediately thereafter. A process to assess your progress on a periodic basis also creates an opportunity for you to regularly review your commitments, adjust your goals, and recommit (Exercise 9.1).

The Critic

It's not that I wouldn't always be committed to my goals; it's just that they wouldn't always be the focus of my attention. Of course I always want to have a better relationship with my kids. Of course I want to be a good leader at work. I used to think that wanting was the same as committing, but I never used to follow through on things I wanted to change about myself. Now I realize that commitment to this kind of change takes time and hard work.

Every week I review my commitments and the actions I am currently working on, and I rededicate myself to them. A couple of times I have added something new to them, but for the most part they have stayed the same. I am committed to having my kids feel comfortable being honest with me. I am committed to having my employees be excited about working for me. To accomplish these things I am committed to telling them about all of the things that they do that I admire, respect, and appreciate. I am also committed to stopping myself from pointing out every single flaw that I see in everyone and everything around me. I certainly have enough flaws of my own.

Just reading these things and saying them again every week really helps me. Then, once per month, I review everything, all of my notes, all of the strategies that I have employed throughout the whole process. I read through it all and plan out the month ahead. This is too important to me to let it slide. I know I could slip right back into my old patterns. It took me a while, but I finally realized that I didn't like who I was. I don't ever want to be that person again. So I'm going to keep on reminding myself how to continue to be the person I am today.

Darrell created a routine to help him renew his commitment every month. If your change is important enough for you to go through the various steps outlined in this book, it is unlikely that your commitment will waver. However, your attention almost certainly will. There will be times when your life is hectic and stressful, when important events draw your concentration away from your commitment to change. It is easy to forget about the actions that have helped you to make change in your life, which is why it is so important to have a regular process for recommitting to both your goals and the activities that support those goals.

The process of recommitting keeps you focused, energized and dedicated to your objectives. It can also be an opportunity to celebrate the positive impact your change is having on your life and your work. Each time Darrell, The Critic, recommitted, he reinforced the tremendous importance of his efforts to his relationships with family members and colleagues. It directed his energy to the actions he needed to continue to take, and it reminded him of how far he had come. Consistent recommitment is a key act on the way to maintaining your change over time. These commitments that you make to yourself may or may not change as you go through this process. Whatever changes do come about should occur as a result of a conscious choice, not casual neglect (Excercise 9.2).

Exercise 9.2   Recommit

Build a routine to determine your commitments.
- Once per month review your materials and commitments from Steps 1, 2, and 3 and (as needed) adjust your commitments.
- Identify with whom you will discuss this and seek input.

Be sure to schedule time in your calendar and/or leave yourself reminders to complete these actions.

Make It Easier

Even with the best-laid plans you will still make some mistakes. Some of the decisions you make in this process will miss the mark. You will identify and eliminate the causes of your old behaviors, only to discover that there are other causes you hadn't recognized. You will design cues to remind you to engage in your new behavior and find that they don't actually remind you to do anything. This is a trial and error process. There is no foolproof plan. However, assessing your progress creates the opportunity for you to identify the best and worst parts of your plan and make adjustments as you go.

The Pushover

I set up a routine in which I consistently asked myself what worked and what didn't. Where were my techniques working and where not? As I looked at some of my successes it helped me to see that it really was helpful for me to delay my decisions. One of the strongest influences on my behavior was feeling pressure to make a decision. Even in group meetings it forced me to act. Whenever someone asked for a volunteer and there was silence in the room I felt an enormous pressure to act at that moment. Once I recognized how much time pressure influenced my behavior, I was able to focus more attention on ways that I could limit or eliminate the effects of that pressure.

It also helped me to realize how much more likely I was to revert to old behaviors when I wasn't allowed to delay. Overall, I was

> having a lot of success. I didn't volunteer as much in group settings and I made fewer commitments in one-on-one discussions. However, the more I watched and evaluated my progress, the more I realized that when someone told me they needed an answer immediately I always caved. In general I had improved dramatically, but when this particular circumstance arose, I went right back to my bad habits.

By reviewing her actions Karen realized where her strategies were working and where she could benefit from some new ideas. Once she realized that, she was able to go back to the drawing board to develop new techniques to help her through those situations. However, she never would have seen the pattern in her behavior if she hadn't used a consistent routine for evaluating her actions.

It is highly unlikely that you will get everything perfect the first time you try to break a self-addiction. As a professional coach there are many techniques that I believe are highly effective that I have tried to impart throughout this book. However, none of these techniques work all of the time or for all people. Your experience still has to tell you what is effective and what isn't, and that goes for every part of your change process.

You should not only be looking at the actions you determined in the last two chapters. You should also assess the effectiveness of who you have invited to support you and how you have utilized that support. Making your change easier entails looking at all aspects of your efforts to evaluate how you can better inspire and shape your new behavior going forward. Remember that you are engaged in an iterative process. You want to refine your actions to make them more and more effective as you go (Exercise 9.3).

Sustain Your Change

You've worked very hard up to this point. However, it does get easier. Think about the road you have traveled. Someone once popularized the notion that it takes 21 days to break an old habit. I'm not sure how they defined habit, but I know that that doesn't hold true

---

Exercise 9.3 Review Your Process

Continue with the review process that you created in Step 6 to assess and adjust your support. Also, every month answer these questions about the action strategies you developed in Steps 7 and 8:

- Where/when have I had my best and worst results? What makes these situations different?

- What new strategies can I employ to improve my results?

Once you have answered the questions above, where necessary, discuss changes you would like to make with your supporters and implement new strategies to make your actions more effective.

---

for self-addiction. Some may take less time, some more, but there is no set time limit after which you will be "cured" and never have to think about the behavior again. Breaking a self-addiction entails building new skills and creating new routines, which takes time.

It begins with a great deal of vigilance. You have to watch yourself. You have to prepare for various situations so that you are on your toes, ready to exhibit your new, more desirable behaviors. You have to slow down your responses in situations where you are at risk of falling into the old, undesirable behaviors. You dedicate a significant portion of your mental energy and overall attention to breaking your addiction.

Eventually, that alertness reduces as you gain confidence in your new self. You can exercise your new behaviors casually, almost without thinking about them. Sometimes you almost slip and, in your recovery, recommit to staying away from the addictive behavior. You feel truly free.

When your new behaviors become part of your routine, they are truly a part of you. You can breathe easier and relax your monitoring and self-evaluation. However, you should not give it up altogether. Once you may have had to scrutinize your behavior daily or weekly in order to break your addiction. When those daily and weekly reports consistently return positive results, it will be time for you to move into the next phase. At that point you may wish to revisit the behavior monthly or every 3-6 months to ensure that you don't relapse and slip back into old patterns without noticing.

The Worker

It's been two years now since I started to make this effort in earnest. I am happy to say that things have gone pretty well. It's not that it wasn't difficult or doesn't continue to be tough at times, but I spend a lot more time with my family now. I make it to the important events. For the most part I am able to separate my work time and my home time.

One thing that I do now to keep that going is that I set up a new routine with my husband. Every three months or so we go on vacation. Sometimes we include the kids, sometimes not. Sometimes we go away on a big trip. Sometimes we just go to a bed and breakfast for the weekend, but before each trip we sit down and talk about the last three months. We talk about the important events we've had as a family. We talk about the time we have spent together, and we make sure that I've stuck to my new routines.

Most of these discussions have been positive. A couple of times my husband has pushed me to be more vigilant in my efforts. Then we go away on vacation. I allow myself to enjoy my time with my family, and on the way back, whether on the plane or in our car, I study my notes. Everything I have done throughout this process I've captured in a single notebook, and I read it cover to cover on my way home from my vacations.

I look at the original reasons I wrote down to make the change, the commitments I've made during the process, the input I've gotten from people around me, and all of the strategies I've used to build my new behaviors. It's actually quite soothing and reassuring to see how hard I've worked to change and how far I've come. In fact, sometimes I can't even believe that my notes describe me. It's almost like I'm reading someone else's diary when I take these times to look back at how I was. When I'm done, I feel energized and ready to get back to my job, but also to continue to work at getting home from my job.

Far from being an onerous task, Susan's review of her notes from her change process was a personally fulfilling and even pleasing experience. Through this process she realized the depth of her commitment and the personal power she had to overcome challenges in her life. It also kept her honest and maintained the progress she had made. Deeply ingrained behaviors don't just go away. Unfortunately, breaking a self-addiction is not an item that you can check off of your to-do list and assume it will never resurface. You will need to monitor yourself to ensure that you keep your new behaviors going.

You should enter the monitoring phase once you have seen your old behaviors disappear and your new behaviors stabilize, meaning you shouldn't be experiencing any relapses. Your new behaviors should feel comfortable to you and you shouldn't feel strong urges anymore for your old self-addiction. Reaching this point takes different lengths of time depending on the behavior and the individual. If you relapse quite a bit, then stick with the activities outlined earlier in this chapter for a longer time, perhaps six to twelve months. If you find that your new behaviors have stuck with you pretty easily, then you may be able to shift to maintenance after two or three months.

The maintenance phase of change is simply a process to remind you of what you have done and ensure that you haven't slipped. The next exercise is akin to performing all of the previous activities in this chapter, but on a less regular basis.

Exercise 9.4   Maintain Your Change

Schedule a time in the next 3-12 months to perform the following maintenance check-in:
- Reread all of your notes from Steps 1–9.
- Evaluate whether or not you have maintained your progress.
  - If so, commit to your next maintenance check-in and schedule it on your calendar.
  - If not, return to the commitments, supporters and actions that you utilized to make the change.

Include someone else in this process for perspective and support.

Circle of Action

This is the end of your third Circle of Strength. You created routines to surround yourself with (actions) and reminders to support your change. You monitored yourself to improve your understanding of your self-addictions and formulate strategies to break them. You have shaped your behavior by altering your environment and preparing yourself. You have built schedules to consistently bring you back to your efforts.

As with the Circle of Support and the Circle of Awareness, the Circle of Action is powerful when it is a consistent force in your life. The strength you draw from it comes from the regularity with which you return to it. Breaking a self-addiction is a challenging task. You are bound to have some successes and some setbacks along the way. The Circle of Action keeps you in a cycle to make progress, evaluate your results, adjust your approach, and repeat the process as many times as it takes to get it right.

Now is the time for congratulations! If you have fully created your three Circles of Strength and conquered your self-addiction, you deserve high praise. Even if you haven't completed all of the action steps yet, now you should have dramatically increased your understanding of how to change yourself. At the beginning of this book I said that it wouldn't be easy. However, with the right approach you can surround yourself with the understanding, the people, and the routines you need to make your change a reality. Hopefully, you are well on your way to breaking your self-addiction, if not already there. Your journey is almost complete. In the final chapter you will look at what's next for you now that you have undertaken this phenomenal effort.

Moving Onward

Questions to get you started:

How far have you come?

Where is your next destination?

Renee is now a health nut all year round. She avoids the gym in January because it is too crowded with the New Year's Health Nuts, but she knows that by February they will have forgotten their New Year's resolutions to stay in shape, given up on their exercise crusades, and disappeared from the gym until next year.

Denise is a recovering "control freak." She now lives by the mantra that other people should be free to make their own decisions.

Jonathan hasn't won Manager of the Year honors, but his team now likes him as a manager. He has dramatically reduced his criticizing behavior and even compliments people on a regular basis.

What accomplishment do Renee, Denise, and Jonathan share? Each has conquered his or her self-addiction. They fought hard, worked for what was important to them, and made their lives and the lives of people around them better in the process.

You now have a powerful tool for changing yourself, one which can greatly enrich your life. These riches may or may not be in the form of money. Regardless of their makeup, they are extremely valuable. They might take the form of better relationships, better health, greater happiness, or a better career. What if you could have all of those things? What would it be like if you were able to change at will? You know what you want to be. What if you had a system to identify the important changes you want to make, adapt your behaviors as needed, and sustain those changes over time? I hope that you are thrilled with the realization that you now have that system.

I recently spoke to a woman who was incapable of surrendering control. We spoke at length about things she had done, behaviors she exhibited and events that caused her to realize that she had a problem. Her controlling behavior was causing problems for her at home and at work, and at one point she broke down and cried, "I know all of that. I've been through this before. What do I do?"

We spoke for a while and outlined an initial course of action. I don't yet know if she will do the work necessary to change, but her plea echoes a frustration felt by so many people who have tried in vain to improve themselves and their lives. Unfortunately, they just didn't know how to change.

The book that you hold in your hand offers the answer to the question, "How?" You now have a set of steps that you can take to make just about any change you want to make. If you have already followed them successfully, then you know their power and will use them again. These steps are my answer to the frustration of change and the cry of, "What do I do?"

What should you do next?

As we near the end of our journey, I hope that you have found it valuable and satisfying. However, before we conclude, consider three more questions:

1. Whom should you thank?
2. Whom can you help?
3. What's next?

Whom should you thank?

As I get close to the completion of this book, I find myself thinking more and more about the Acknowledgments section of the book. I never used to read those pages, but now I find them interesting and exciting. I've always viewed authors as Lone-Ranger types slugging away at their keyboards, overcoming all of their obstacles on their own. Initially I couldn't see how I would fill up the one or two pages that authors typically dedicate to thanking people. Now I realize that many, many people supported me and lifted me up throughout the process.

I have the luxury of the Acknowledgments section in which I can thank people. However, you don't need anything as formal as that to express your appreciation to those who have helped you on your journey.

Exercise   Offer Acknowledgments

Make a list of all of the people who have helped you in your change process and then determine how you will thank them. Will you mail a hand-written note, deliver a gift basket, take them to lunch or dinner, or drop off a personalized gift? Once you decide how you will show your appreciation, act immediately. The longer you wait, the easier it is to let this important part of the process slide.

You have a community of supporters who want you to succeed and have been willing to put in their time and energy to help you along the way. This is your opportunity to show them just how much they have meant to you.

Whom can you help?

When I found my publisher for this book, I discovered that several people I knew were also trying to write their own books. They had questions and wanted advice on how to go about securing a publisher. I was happy to share any secrets I knew. These acquaintances of mine were good people who were struggling with an extremely challenging task. It made me feel terrific to know that I was helping them out.

I hope you have now reached a certain level of success in your efforts, and that the time has come when you can help others. Supporting other people in their changes has benefits. First, by supporting others you will increase their goodwill toward you and the likelihood that they will support you in the future. Second, by coaching someone else through the change process you will improve your own understanding of the process and increase your ability to effectively use it in the future. As the saying goes, "If you want to truly know something, teach it." Last, but not least, by helping others you will improve the lives of people around you. That should be worthwhile in and of itself.

The challenge when you help others to change is that you can't impose your will on them. They have to want to make the change for themselves. What you need to do is find people who are ready for the support you can provide. The key is to offer your support, and then let them guide you. The best place to make this offer is to the people who have supported you (Exercise: Support Others).

What's next?

After doing all of this work some people can't wait to get to their next personal project, others prefer to take a break. This is a mat-

---

Exercise   Support Others

For each of your supporters, perform the following:

- Thank them for their help.

- Ask them if there is anything they are working on changing in themselves.

- Offer to support them in their change process.

Once someone is interested in your help, look at the different types of partners that were described in Step 4. Review these different options with the person you are helping and determine with him how you can best support his change.

---

ter of choice, and there is certainly no best way. A friend of mine recently got a new job. She had been working in the same place for four years and decided that she wanted a different experience. She got a new job that sounded fun and interesting, and she was excited to start. She finished up her old job on a Friday and reported at her new employer at eight o'clock sharp on Monday morning. She just couldn't wait to move on to the next thing.

Personally, I would have asked my new employer for a couple of weeks off before starting the new job. I don't know how I would have spent that time. Perhaps I would have done some work around the house. Maybe I just would have relaxed and caught up on some reading, or I would have taken a vacation and gone somewhere fun. After four years of dedicating my brain power to one place, one group of people and problems, I would have taken some time to let my brain rest.

You have now dedicated a lot of time and brain power to breaking your self-addiction. I hope that you have succeeded or are well on your way to completing that journey. You have also learned a process that you can use to lead yourself through change in the future. When the time comes that you feel you have overcome your self-addiction perhaps you will be like my friend. A day or two later you will identify your next self-addiction and begin the process again. If you are like me, you will give yourself more of a break. Take some time off and get some rest. Then you can begin again.

Either way, there is something that you should do first. You have worked so hard and hopefully achieved so much. It is time to celebrate. However you celebrate, take the opportunity now to be proud of what you have accomplished, and do something special for yourself.

A Final Note

The Talker

It's hard for me to describe how I feel after all of this work. It isn't often that I'm left speechless. I think I'm happy and generally relieved. The changes I have made have improved my family life. I think my wife is happier with how I listen to her now, and I think other people, friends and family, appreciate it, too. I can also see that people are more comfortable with me at work.

The improved relationships make me happy, but more than anything, I'm relieved. I think it was actually quite a burden to always try to be the entertainer. It wasn't until I changed that I realized how much easier my life could be. Now I can sit back and relax. I can let things go. I can allow discussions to go where other people take them and be happy with the outcomes and with myself.

Now I find myself going with the flow. I'm less tense in group meetings. I'm more casual and comfortable in one-on-one discussions. I'm simply relieved. I didn't really know what I would get when I started. I had this shocking experience where I suddenly realized, "Wow! I have to change," but I didn't really understand what it would mean to me. Now I know. The prize when I made it through the maze isn't talking less. It isn't improving my chances of promotion at work. The prize is that I'm more relaxed around other people and happier with myself.

As you conquer a self-addiction, you may find that in the process you let go of tension that you didn't even know you had. What's more important, you may become happier with yourself in general. In the process of breaking your self-addiction you certainly make an important change to your behavior, but that is not all that you accomplish. You also find reserves of personal strength that you didn't know existed. You discover the caring and supportive nature of people and realize that you have terrific supporters all around you.

I hope you feel happier and stronger as a result of this process. I encourage you to continue to use it and to share it with others. When you are successful, celebrate. When you fall short of your goals, admit it and realize that mistakes are part of the learning process, then adjust and do better next time. Remember that self-addiction is doing the same thing over and over again, knowing you'll get the same bad results. You now know how to break the cycle and gain the good results you want. The choice is up to you. Good luck making your next change.

Recommended Reading

Following is a list of books I have found helpful either in the writing of this book or in my own self-development.

Crucial Conversations, by Kerry Patterson et al., for discussing challenging, emotional or awkward topics

Authentic Happiness, by Martin E. P. Seligman, for living a happier life

The 7 Powers of Questions, by Dorothy Leeds, for asking more and better questions

It's Your Ship, by Captain D. Michael Abrashoff, for general leadership

Primal Leadership, by Daniel Goleman, Richard Boyatzis and Annie McKee, for leading with emotional intelligence

Getting Things Done, by David Allen, for personal productivity and time management

Changing for Good, by James Prochaska, John Norcross, and Carlo DiClemente, for understanding behavior change

Mastering Self-Leadership, by Charles Manz, for personal effectiveness

The Power of Now, by Eckhart Tolle, for living in the moment

Taming Your Gremlin, by Rick Carson, for freeing yourself from self-defeating behaviors and beliefs

A Yellow Raft in Blue Water, by Michael Dorris, for understanding the power of shifting your perspective

Three Deep Breaths, by Thomas Crum, for managing stress and anger

Resources for Traditional Addictions

Following is a list of websites for organizations that provide support for many traditional addictions.

Alcoholics Anonymous—www.aa.org

Gamblers Anonymous—www.gamblersanonymous.org

Sexaholics Anonymous—www.sa.org

Overeaters Anonymous—www.oa.org

Cocaine Anonymous—www.ca.org

Narcotics Anonymous—www.na.org

Index

About the Author

Noah Blumenthal is the founder and president of Leading Principles, Inc., a consulting company specializing in executive coaching, leadership, and team development. As a consultant and coach, he has worked with corporations, not-for-profit, and educational institutions including MetLife, Bank of America, Pfizer, Johnson & Johnson, Accenture, Leo Burnett, First Energy Corp, New School University, and Fairfield University. Noah has coached hundreds of executives on making difficult changes and has trained new and seasoned coaches, HR leaders, executives, and managers in the art of coaching. He studied psychology as an undergraduate student at Brandeis University and organizational psychology as a graduate student at Columbia University. Noah is a renowned speaker and workshop leader delivering talks on changing ingrained behaviors, building executive teams, and developing effective interpersonal relationships.

Noah's experiences have left him with a powerful belief that people are better than their actions and can be happier than they are. They simply need the tools to change what they want to change. To find out about additional tools for change, visit www.Youre AddictedToYou.com.

To learn more about Noah's coaching, keynote speeches, and workshops, contact him at Leading Principles, Inc., P.O. Box 876, New Hyde Park, NY 11040. Phone: 516-352-2744. E-mail: Noah@LeadingPrinciples.com. Or visit his website: www.LeadingPrinciples.com.

About Berrett-Koehler Publishers

Berrett-Koehler is an independent publisher dedicated to an ambitious mission: Creating a World that Works for All.

We believe that to truly create a better world, action is needed at all levels—individual, organizational, and societal. At the individual level, our publications help people align their lives with their values and with their aspirations for a better world. At the organizational level, our publications promote progressive leadership and management practices, socially responsible approaches to business, and humane and effective organizations. At the societal level, our publications advance social and economic justice, shared prosperity, sustainability, and new solutions to national and global issues.

A major theme of our publications is "Opening Up New Space." They challenge conventional thinking, introduce new ideas, and foster positive change. Their common quest is changing the underlying beliefs, mindsets, and structures that keep generating the same cycles of problems, no matter who our leaders are or what improvement programs we adopt.

We strive to practice what we preach—to operate our publishing company in line with the ideas in our books. At the core of our approach is stewardship, which we define as a deep sense of responsibility to administer the company for the benefit of all of our "stakeholder" groups: authors, customers, employees, investors, service providers, and the communities and environment around us.

We are grateful to the thousands of readers, authors, and other friends of the company who consider themselves to be part of the "BK Community." We hope that you, too, will join us in our mission.

A BK Life Book

This book is part of our BK Life series. BK Life books change people's lives. They help individuals improve their lives in ways that are beneficial for the families, organizations, communities, nations, and world in which they live and work. To find out more, visit www.bk-life.com.

Be Connected

Visit Our Website

Go to www.bkconnection.com to read exclusive previews and excerpts of new books, find detailed information on all Berrett-Koehler titles and authors, browse subject-area libraries of books, and get special discounts.

Subscribe to Our Free E-Newsletter

Be the first to hear about new publications, special discount offers, exclusive articles, news about bestsellers, and more! Get on the list for our free e-newsletter by going to www.bkconnection.com.

Participate in the Discussion

To see what others are saying about our books and post your own thoughts, check out our blogs at www.bkblogs.com.

Get Quantity Discounts

Berrett-Koehler books are available at quantity discounts for orders of ten or more copies. Please call us toll-free at (800) 929-2929 or email us at bkp.orders@aidcvt.com.

Host a Reading Group

For tips on how to form and carry on a book reading group in your workplace or community, see our website at www.bkconnection. com.

Join the BK Community

Thousands of readers of our books have become part of the "BK Community" by participating in events featuring our authors, reviewing draft manuscripts of forthcoming books, spreading the word about their favorite books, and supporting our publishing program in other ways.

If you would like to join the BK Community, please contact us at bkcommunity@bkpub.com.